MW00947583

Marathon Training Mindset

The Ultimate Guide to Fostering
Mental Strength, Breaking
Physical Barriers, and Performing
Your Best While Being One With
Your Mind and Body When
Training for a Marathon

By Phoenix S.

© Copyright 2023 - All rights reserved.

The content contained within this book may not be reproduced, duplicated or transmitted without direct written permission from the author or the publisher.

Under no circumstances will any blame or legal responsibility be held against the publisher, or author, for any damages, reparation, or monetary loss due to the information contained within this book, either directly or indirectly.

Legal Notice:

This book is copyright protected. It is only for personal use. You cannot amend, distribute, sell, use, quote or paraphrase any part, or the content within this book, without the consent of the author or publisher.

Disclaimer Notice:

Please note the information contained within this document is for educational and entertainment purposes only. All effort has been executed to present accurate, up to date, reliable, complete information. No warranties of any kind are declared or implied. Readers acknowledge that the author is not engaged in the rendering of legal, financial, medical or professional advice. The content within this book has been derived from various sources. Please consult a licensed professional before attempting any techniques outlined in this book.

By reading this document, the reader agrees that under no circumstances is the author responsible for any losses, direct or indirect, that are incurred as a result of the use of the information contained within this document, including, but not limited to, errors, omissions, or inaccuracies.

Table of Contents

Introduction

Chapter Outline

- From the Neolithic Ages to the present day

- Development of fitness in the United States of America

- Introduction of physical education in government schools

- Evolving into a commercial industry

- Positive mindset is necessary to overcome a marathon

- Running to great lengths

- Anyone can run a marathon

The History of Exercise to Improve Body Fitness: Progress From the Neolithic Ages to Now

What is Physical Fitness?

A person is regarded as physically fit when they are capable of carrying out daily activities without getting tired easily. Fitness, therefore, measures the ability of the body to function effectively and with maximum efficiency in carrying out duties such as household chores, recreational activities, and workplace responsibilities. While health professionals will use standard metrics to assure the wellbeing of an individual, the ordinary person will rely on the ability to perform daily activities without the body suffering from fatigue and memory lapses.

Sember V & Morrison S (2018) characterizes physical activity as a behavior that is influenced by elements that operate on four levels. These levels are classified as the physiological, psychological, ecological, and sociocultural categories. At the psychological level, the body reacts to thoughts which are referred to as the 'mind-body connection'. The psychological level embraces the mental strength required for exercise. Muscle strength and endurance are classified under the physiological aspect. It is these two aspects that are rigorously put to the test when you run a marathon. While the ecological and sociocultural aspects will influence your running, their effect is peripheral to warrant inclusion in this book.

Development of Running Through the Neolithic Ages to Present Day

According to Cachola, M (2021), as early as 10, 000 B.C., exercise has been a way of life for our forefathers, as seen with the intense activities that they would regularly do such as making shelter and hunting. Further to that, when a project had been successfully completed, the ancestors would gather around a fire, dancing and celebrating the success. As we progressed through the Neolithic Ages (from 8,000 B.C. to the year 2,000 B.C.) people started cultivating fertile soils in order to achieve agricultural productivity. Exercise, thus, became part of life. The growing population brought with it the need for more farming activities, as people started storing food for their households.

With civilization, new ways of attaining physical fitness were unintentionally pursued. The new era brought with it a series of wars between countries that required men to be physically fit in order to battle. With the progression of civilization, the military strength of nations influenced the fitness of men. In Ancient Greece, there was an understanding that having a physically fit body meant that the mind is healthy. Further to that, the Greeks believed that physical wellness positively influenced emotional health.

When the Romans conquered the Greeks, they pursued a pleasant lifestyle with the belief that life revolves around pleasure. This lifestyle led to an unhealthy army, and eventually together with the Greeks, they were conquered by the Barbarians who were physically fit. It was during the rule by the Barbarian tribes that the Greek norms of fitness were restored. The teaching of physical education started to spread among societies during this Dark Age (the 900 years between the fifth century and the 14th century). This can be attributed to the birth of modern physical fitness history.

History of Physical Fitness in the United States of America (USA)

During the Colonial Era in the USA, the authorities went about building an economy based on agriculture. This brought with it physical hardships for the population. Americans did not need to train in order to attain fitness because their manual tilling lifestyle ensured they were fit. As the nation grew, European immigrants influenced the ideals of physical fitness immensely. The new nation's leaders reinforced the idea of consistent running or swimming as a way of sustaining the fitness of the body. The fitness regime was also extended to women during this time.

Unfortunately, the Americans turned to an inactive way of life during the Industrial Revolution. This revolution in manufacturing occurred mainly in the United States of America and Europe during the period ca 1760 to about 1840. The lack of physical activity, unfortunately, carried with it a lot of fitness-related ailments such as diabetes and hypertension. When the authorities introduced military drafting, many Americans were exposed due to the negative effects of inactivity.

As the population struggled with diseases, the authorities introduced physical education in schools. Physical Education came with two branches of physical fitness; namely, a workout to attain fitness and an exercise in order to compete in sporting activities. Coupled with physical activity in schools, the fitness industry slowly became commercial throughout the 20th century, as the population replaced the sedentary way of life with formalized workouts and sporting activities.

The industry has, thus, become commercial with a lot of money being made both in the mainstream fitness industry and the support sectors such as sports apparel.

Significance of a Positive Attitude in Marathon Training

A positive attitude can be explained as an optimistic mind. In this state, the mind is encouraged to overcome whatever situations you are facing. The mind approaches interactions with people constructively and with confidence.

According to Jaeshke A et al (2020), a successful marathoner needs to overcome certain psychological barriers in order to complete a run. The obstacles start with taking in air at the first jog to exhaling during the last two miles of a marathon. Overcoming the pain and fatigue will require a positive mind. If you do not think you will overcome the challenging barriers, they may not be able to achieve a lot of the goals they set. A positive mind is adventurous and will set out to achieve said goals.

Running a marathon is a grueling task; one that will demand a confident approach, and a mind that sticks to the adventure however strong the challenges are. A negative mind will give up part-way through the task of running the race when the race demands you continue to mount.

Research has shown that when you feel tired and your muscles are complaining, your body may actually not be fatigued to that extent. Rather, the brain may be receiving a variety of messages. So, when you are running, you might need to condition your mind to handle the situations when the brain wants to give up.

Setting Marathon Goals to Achieve Greatness

While many runners focus primarily on enjoying the run, other marathoners reap other benefits from the sport that include controlling weight, promoting heart and mental health, and many others.

Operationally, achieving a goal for a runner could be defined as successfully completing the race course in a time that is below or equal to the set time. However, the goals that most marathoners set go beyond running within the targeted time that they set. A greater number of habitual marathoners run for fun and for the health benefits associated with running. The goal will usually revolve around a person becoming the best copy of one's self. People who usually attain their best version exhibit high levels of confidence, which usually brings success in many areas of life.

Can Anyone Train and Run a Marathon?

Anyone who is healthy, active, and full of life can take to the road and run a marathon. However, it is true that the greater part of the population will see 26.2 miles as an impossible distance to cover. What you would need as a novice is the correct will to run a marathon, a proper guideline for training, dedication to the training plan, and the perseverance to successfully cross the finishing line of a marathon.

The Content Covered in This Manuscript

This eBook is a guide that you may use when you want to raise your mental strength so that you can overcome physical obstacles and perform to your best. In trying to equip the novice, the book offers methods you may pursue in order to adopt a habit of running. It assists the reader in understanding the ways running can be used to overcome anxiety and lessen stress levels and other various health benefits that come with running a marathon. Preparing you to live a life of day-to-day running, the manuscript will assist in taking you away from the couch and onto the race course by exposing you to the various proven techniques that runners use to successfully complete that 26.2-mile run. The concept of running should be viewed from the aspect of minimizing the chances of injury to the body and improving cardiovascular health.

The book will help you embrace a rewarding sport that develops you into a well-organized, target-oriented, effectual, and intelligent athlete. It will assist you to place emphasis on attaining goals that are classified as shrewd, enjoyable to achieve, and planned to be achievable on organized training programs. Covering topics on the correct mental preparation required to run and building the essential stamina, the manuscript guides you through to proper ways of converting running into your habit. The content covered in this book includes proper nutrition to be taken when you prepare to run a marathon and the importance of hydrating the body with both salts and water. The guidelines laid out consist of the various techniques that you may adopt when running and strategies to follow in order to rest the body and mind appropriately.

Chapter 1:

The Right Approach to Start Running

Chapter overview

- Capabilities of individuals to run

- Benefits of a positive attitude

- Managing Imposter Syndrome

- How to prepare the mind

- Overcoming mental obstacles

Categories of People According to Running Capabilities

This manuscript will run with the theme that everyone is capable of running a 26.2-mile race. However, when you consider that people will have approaches to running that are different, runners can be grouped into various categories. The categories below attempt to group individuals according to their reasons and their capacities to run.

Types of people who run:

- Mental blocks can prevent people from running. There will be people who consider running as punishment. In sports, coaches usually impose running on athletes as punishment. This can create a mental block in people who have been subjected to this form of punishment. These people may block running completely with a mindset that they are not athletic or not well-coordinated to run.

- Certain individuals will be indifferent to the sport of running. This group will run half-heartedly with regular stops. The habit is usually exercised by people who are chasing unrealistic goals such as trying to please somebody.

- There will be people who run because they enjoy running. For this group, they enjoy synchronizing their breathing, pacing, and their strides.

- There will be individuals who enjoy the running ritual. The group could be likened to beer drinkers and smokers who enjoy their habits with friends and in particular situations like celebratory gatherings. People who enjoy the ritual of running might enjoy running in a group with certain friends, running along particular routes they enjoy, wearing the latest gear, etc. They probably don't like running that much, but they adore a routine that they associate with the race.

- Then, there are groups that enjoy the benefits that come with running. For a long time, running has been associated with providing good health to the body. Running will particularly help with making sleep enjoyable and reducing stress levels. Some of the results of running include making the runner feel confident and providing an energy and fitness boost. Running may also assist an individual to compensate for the guilt of eating junk food. For other runners, running allows them to be active when playing with their children.

Types of people who do not run:

- People that miss running because they were forced to quit the habit. It could be due to injury, advanced age, and/or a temporary medical condition.

- Individuals who quit running and have no regrets for stopping. This may be because their career is over or they participated for the wrong reasons.

- Some people will never run, nor will they enjoy the races because they have a medical condition. For example, when you have a severe heart condition or a critical asthma condition, your physician might discourage you from running.

There may, however, be more groups, and runners may also overlap into the different categories.

The Need for a Positive Attitude in Running a Marathon

In order to attain success in any task you undertake to perform, the correct mindset is to always approach the execution with a positive attitude. If you have sound emotional health, you will be cautious of what your mind is thinking, alert to your feelings, and can control your behavior. Your mind will adjust to ways of coping with high stress levels and you will be able to treat challenges in life as situations that have to be confronted.

The Influence of Positive Thinking for Marathoners

Thinking negatively will prevent you from reaching your maximum performance. If you keep thinking phrases such as, "I will not complete the race," that thinking is harmful to your race. Studies have proved that if you adopt a positive mindset, you will clearly improve in performance and also increase your chances of recovering quickly.

Reframing Your Thoughts

This technique identifies ways in which you perceive situations in order to think positively. All runners will, at times, think irrationally, particularly when the race day is nearing, and will start to get paranoid about it. Once you ditch the negative thoughts, you start to identify the good aspects of the upcoming race. The listing below is a detail of some of the ideas that may assist you to inject a level of positivity into your brain for use in training daily. Examples of reframing negative thoughts are:

- Negative thought: I don't have enough endurance to complete a marathon. Reframed to: I might not have the endurance to last for 26.2 miles, but I have a feeling that everyone in this race is looking up to me.

- Negative thought: I am not a marathon runner. Reframed to: I am a developing runner who will continue training to run until I achieve my objectives.

Rely on Positive Affirmations

When you substitute statements like, "I will not complete the race today," with positive phrases like, "I will make it," it will help to realign the mind into thinking positively. Positive affirmations can help turn around the negative internal communications in your brain. Practicing these can assist in activating the reward system in your mind. This will boost your confidence, empower you, and encourage your faith.

Keep a Log of the Positives

One negative side is that the situation can easily overwhelm the numerous positives that fall on your side. Keeping a log of the positive circumstances that you meet will help you in overcoming the negatives that might fall on you. Make a habit of moving around with the notebook or putting it by your bedside when you sleep.

Set Realistic Race Goals

You will reach a high level of motivation when you set short-term and long-stretching goals that are within your reach. Do not run into the risk of demotivating yourself by setting objectives that professionals would otherwise target. Set SMART goals:

Specific: Ask yourself the question; Am I targeting defined race goals?

Measurable: Can the goals be measurable? E.g., complete the marathon within a set time. How do I know I have achieved the goal?

Attainable: Are my goals within reach? E.g., have I set times which are not even achievable by professionals?

Realistic: Do I have the financial/material resources and enough time to dedicate to attaining these goals?

Timeliness: When do I intend to start training to run in a local summer marathon?

Never Look Back with Regret

Do not dwell on unsuccessful attempts. When you reflect on your training exercises, don't forget the best times that you achieved in training, the hill you conquered, and always remember the successes you achieved. In summary, always look at the brighter side of things.

Leverage on Past Achievements

If you have run a successful marathon before, you are likely to be confident to reach your objective once again. Success is generally known to give birth to another achievement.

Managing Imposter Syndrome in Marathon Running

The Negative Side of Imposter Syndrome

Imposter syndrome, also called 'impostorism', is a psychological phenomenon in individuals whereby a person persistently internalizes fear, doubts her past achievements, and is uncertain about their skills and talents. The feelings of restlessness, nervousness, negative self-talk, depression, and anxiety may be symptoms of imposter syndrome.

Male runners, those that consistently achieve, and individuals who are perfectionists are more vulnerable to the syndrome as compared to female athletes. Imposter syndrome can negatively affect your attitude to the extent that you lose self-confidence. It may also lead to disappointing performance, setting objectives that are beyond your capacity, emotional fatigue, self-sabotage, and general dissatisfaction with running. The first step in order to manage imposter syndrome is to ascertain whether you possess the syndrome or not. If your responses to the following questions are positive, then you are most likely an imposter.

You will need to assess the syndrome by answering these simple questions:

- Are you free to accept praise?

- Do you show your confidence to other runners?

- Do you train beyond your limits?

- Are you fearful of success?

- Do you compare your challenges to other people?

- Do you doubt your abilities?

- Are you not focusing a lot on past performances?

- Do you feel your success was overrated?

- Are you shy to run with your colleagues because you feel they will discuss your performance?

- Do you compare your performance to your running mates? If you answered "yes" to most of these, you could have imposter syndrome.

Ways to Overcome Imposter Syndrome

The following are the recommendations you may follow so that you deal with imposter syndrome. It does not matter whether you are a professional or a recreational runner, answering these questions in your mind will help ascertain your attitude.

- Talk to your training mates or people that will understand you. Open up about your feelings, including your responses to the questions above. Listen to the advice they propose.

- It is impossible for any runner to attain perfectionism. You may only approach perfectionism. Assess your potential and accept it as your target. Reaching your genuine potential should form the basis of your running goals. Don't waste energy by trying to perform to the level of someone else running next to you. So, try to convince yourself to stop wasting your energy while striving to be the admired runner.

- Contest your thinking that you are not a born marathoner, your past achievements are not genuine, and running is not for you. You need to pay attention to the results and internalize them as real.

- You will need to extract lessons from failure. Don't feel ashamed about it. Address the lessons learned by mapping a clear roadmap on how you will overcome the shortcomings, both in training and in the races to come.

- You are not going to attain your running potential as quickly as you might think. The sport is a slow-growth game that needs a lot of patience. Accept the outcomes graciously and prepare to move on without any regrets.

- When you create a picture in your mind of the following images, you are likely to set yourself up for success in the marathon:

  o Yourself successfully completing the race.

  o People who will be cheering you when you are crossing the line.

  o The exact time the clock will read when you cross the finishing line.

  o The sounds coming from the cheering crowds.

  o Your feeling of successfully completing the race.

  o Your close friends congratulating you when you have completed the race.

  o The picture of an exhausted you walking to the bus or car after the marathon.

Professional runners have confirmed visualization as a good tactic to increase performance.

- Compensating yourself with a reward will help you in managing impostorism. This will break the cycle of writing off your achievements, as by celebrating the accomplishment, you are validating it. The rewards could be a simple massage after a tough workout, eating out with the family, or a drive to the countryside on a rest day.

- You may consult a behavioral therapist for strategies that will help you in dealing with the syndrome. Besides being professional, a therapist will probably have handled similar cases before, and their prescriptions usually work. Stick to a plan that calculates calories needed based on the miles that you are running.

- It is important that you realize that every success begins with you taking the first step. The fear of starting will, however, engulf every runner, including professionals. That understanding will help you know that you are not the only one feeling the syndrome. Training is the only way to replace the syndrome with confidence.

Preparing the Mind

Running in a marathon is neither an easy task, nor a run for fun. Marathon runners put in a lot of time in training while the body is adjusting to blisters, cramps, and fatigue. As you run, muscles start hurting and strengthening at the same time. The marathon is as much a battle for the mind as it is for the body. You will need to stay motivated throughout the preparations for the marathons and when enrolling to participate in marathons. Stress is an enemy of the marathon runner. People who are stressed are either apprehensive or upset, and usually, this is because they have not adjusted to handling stress issues in life and a stressed mind cannot handle a marathon.

The following twelve approaches are recommended when preparing the mind to run in a marathon.

1. Correct your inner voice. Our approach to anything is determined by our inner voice. If your inner feelings are positive, you are most likely going to achieve your goals. The inner voice is critical because when it tells a runner that they are not going to finish a race, his anxiety and fear will be heightened. Directing the inner language makes a runner confident and relaxed when approaching the race.

2. Create a positive visual perception and visualize the good moments. Creating an image of yourself crossing the finishing line gives you a belief that you are going to successfully complete the race. Imagining has the advantage that it puts the mind into rehearsal mode before the actual event. A runner always wants to prime the brain in preparation for the actual event. Because of the rehearsal in the mind, the neurons in the brain are fired up. In the period prior to running, as the marathoner, you need to visualize yourself handling stressful moments well during the race. The focus must be put mainly on practicing the moments that are naturally not on the mind. The movie in my mind should play out the crowd responses during the difficult moments and the

achievement of the small milestones during the race. It will help you create a positive mindset if you create images of your family and friends cheering you to the finish line.

3. Give a new name to the emotion of either excitement or nervousness. Emotions are defined as states of the body that are generated subconsciously. So, without knowing, our bodies respond either positively or negatively to emotions. If you are nervous and your heart is pumping hard, it might be important to rename that emotion as excitement. Physiologically, the emotional state of being nervous is the same as that of being excited. The nervous situation is, therefore, converted into a positive situation that triggers anticipation of excitement for the marathon and induces energy in the runner. It is

always advisable to view issues positively when approaching a big race.

4. Create a mental routine that helps calm your body. If you create a mental routine of repetitive tasks that usually calm the body it can be vital in positioning the mind for difficult periods that the runner will face. Examples of the routines could be reciting a poem and 10 minutes of jumping jacks performed every day prior to the race.

5. Target completing the smaller goals before you embark on the bigger ones. Successfully completing the first mile is important if a runner wants to finish the marathon. If you start by thinking of the finishing line at the end you might not go too far. The safest way is to live in the moment you are at that time and set targets within the distance that you are seeing. It could be half a mile, the next lamppost, the nearest tall building, and so on. This helps in destroying anxiety because you will be staying in the moment and putting your focus on distance.

6. Focus mainly on completing the processes successfully. Champions usually win when they put emphasis on performance. Place focus on the rhythm, movement of the feet, breathing and overcoming the small milestones nearest to you.

7. Block bad thoughts lingering in your mind. It could be a song, reciting a prayer, or something that will distract you from listening to internal

negative thoughts. When you start to feel pain when running, the internal dialogue can be destructive rather than assist you in going forward.

8. Smile because you are having fun and it is only a marathon. The electric nerve pulses in the brain function better when a person is happy. A simple smile will, therefore, stimulate a good race. A person actually performs less when they take marathons seriously.

9. Look up and never down or sideways. Don't allow yourself to look down when running. This will invite pain.

10. You are supposed to learn from past experiences. Consider the results and your general performance of any past performance as learning experiences. Remember to always:

    a. Admit the mistakes you have made in your performance. If the error was made to someone, apologize for it.

    b. Record the mistakes in a 'lesson learned' book and prepare to analyze them.

    c. Listen to feedback.

    d. Prepare an application plan arising from the lesson.

    e. Explain to your mates the lessons you learned.

f. Keep reflecting on the growth you are making.

g. Maintain the learning attitude.

Chapter 2:

Love The Marathon

Chapter summary

- Defining a marathon

- How to develop the habit of running

- The history of recreational running and professional athletes

- Running outside the Olympics

- Marathon motivators

- Running techniques

- Selecting the correcting technique for yourself

What Is Running a Marathon?

A marathon is a long-distance run of 26.2 miles. According to Lortie C (2019), the sport of running is defined as a relatively rapid terrestrial movement. Speed is usually not a criteria when defining the sport because the measure of performance will also include issues of endurance and mental strength in ultra distance running.

Make Marathon Running a Habit

When you perform a task repeatedly, it helps to shape your character. Training will primarily influence this because your individual competitive advantage and abilities are built on performing the key skills repeatedly. Hard work and discipline come from repetition. In the context of this dynamic environment, training for a marathon helps to build an enduring character. Beginning a running habit is one of the easiest, and maybe the least expensive, routes to exercise because you just need willingness and a pair of running shoes to start, or you can even run with your bare feet.

The following tips can help you transform marathon running into your identity, and something you perform consistently.

- Allow yourself to run for the first five minutes. As your body adjusts to the temperature of the environment, your mind will begin to forget that the race is taxing, and your body starts to get into the rhythm.

- You must not sprint but jog yourself into the marathon for the first five minutes. The starting pace should allow you to breathe at a rate where you can converse easily.

- If you are a beginner, start by running small miles of say two to three miles at a maximum frequency of three times a week. As you proceed with your training. You may now add more miles and run more frequently every week.

- You must not increase the miles by more than 10 percent week on week. At the beginning of your training, certain parts of the body, like the knees for example, might rebel against you, as stress is new to them.

- Pay attention to the niggles coming out of your parts of the body. As the niggles start showing up, you might need to rest for about two to three days. This will save you from injuries that can take you away from running for long periods.

- Make use of an application to track the runs. With advancements in technology these days, there are now packages that can compile your marathon statistics, such as the distance, pacing rate, and time. This will help boost your internal motivation. In order to reinforce the habit, reward yourself based on the statistics from the application.

- Reward yourself with a new running kit regularly. Target to renew your running shoes by replacing them with the latest version of Nike or Adidas brands for example. Running accessories will also give you that extra motivation. Make it a point that you have more than one pair of running shoes, changing shoes more often can be a source of motivation. Your training kit must be in the closet and must be the most easily accessible kit to wear.

- The recent running applications have a provision for you to write notes as you run. Allow time to capture the moments that make the run enjoyable; moments like helping an old person cross a busy road or approaching a drinking point where you converge with friends.

- To most people, running is a boring and lonely sport. Your mind will require some entertainment, like music, audiobooks, and podcasts, to break the monotony.

- You will need to target racing in a big race at some point in your life. This will encourage you to run habitually.

- Adhering to the training program must be a ritual.

- You can get a running partner who is a friend. Someone you can converse with and will run at your pace. It is helpful to discuss your running goals and ensure alignment of the goals with your partner.

Once you build running as a habit, you reap the health benefits that come with enduring physical exercise, including sanity of the mind and stress treatment.

Recreational Versus Professional Marathon: A Little History

The official 26.2-miler, the marathon, was established in the 20th century and organized as an Olympic sport 25-miler at the first games in Greece in the year 1896. The distance was increased to 26.2 miles at the intervention of the British Monarchy in 1908 at the London Olympics. The marathon distance stuck for a while until it was standardized in 1921.

The event was confined to the Olympics until 1976 when the New York City marathon attracted runners from all over the world. There are six large marathons that are recognized as the biggest marathons in the world. The six are namely; Tokyo, Boston, London, Berlin, Chicago and New York City. Together, they form the Abbott World Marathon Majors series.

The sport was however reserved for men. Officially, women only started competing in the Boston marathon in 1972. However, the sport was embraced by women as early as 1970, and it grew among the gender during the 1970s as more women competed in marathons. The first all-woman marathon was organized in 1973 on October the 28th. Athletes with disabilities can also participate in marathons. As of today, the sport is now completely inclusive, and marathon running is happening all over the world with America hosting over 1100 races in a year. Most marathons now enroll wheelchair marathoners.

The Difference Between a Recreational Long-distance Runner and a Professional Marathoner

A recreational runner aims to enjoy the marathon. You achieve this by running at a pace that is comfortable for your body, and in doing so, you attain the healthiness that comes with running. Running at a recreational pace avoids the stresses that are associated with racing to win a marathon. Professional marathoners target winning races. They are full-time employees who rely on racing for their income.

The amount and intensity of training differentiates professional runners from long-distance recreational athletes. The training program of a professional athlete is more rigorous, and their exercise plan is usually supervised by a coach.

The History of Marathons Outside the Olympics

Marathon running has exciting stories outside the game's history. While the marathon was first organized in 1896 at the Athens Olympic games, the history of lay people participating in the 26.2-mile race dates back to around that time. Outside the Olympics, the first marathon was organized in 1897 in Boston. This Boston Marathon has stood through the years and it is still one of the biggest races in the world. Women only started participating in the Boston marathon in 1972, 75 years after the first race. Notably, it must be mentioned that women only started running the marathon at an Olympic event much later in 1984 at the Los Angeles Olympics. While the history of women running a marathon in the Olympics is markedly brief, two women are reported to have run the race a few days before the event debuted at the Athens Olympics. The two women who are regarded to have pioneered women running in marathons were the Rovithi sisters, Melpomene and Stamathis. The race has developed from being a sport run by a few to being a sport that is both global and participated in by both males and females.

Motivation to Run

The strongest motivation for a runner comes from the requirement to accomplish the goals that they set to achieve. For most athletes, the marathon is the ultimate test of mental endurance and physical fitness. Our lives are driven by setting goals, and at times, a marathon goal can be as minimum as just completing a race. The extreme end of achievement would then be qualifying for big marathons, like Boston or Berlin, and participating in other elite races.

What Will Motivate You to Run

When the alarm rings to wake you to go for training, it can be tempting to just press the snooze button and retreat back to sleep. It is necessary to have some motivation to beat the lure to disobey. We are motivated by different issues of running, ranging from competition and commitment to the benefits on the body and mental health.

- Allocating money to running can motivate you to commit to completing a race. The heart follows where your money has been spent. Once you spend money, it means whatever obstacle comes your way, whether it's weather conditions or the feeling of abandoning the exercise, you have the motivation to continue.

- If you convince your friend to join you in the marathon program, it can motivate you to run. Peer pressure will urge you and, at times, make it difficult for you to find excuses when you don't feel like participating in training.

- Varying the training schedule can be helpful in avoiding boredom as a result of monotonous activities. In order to keep you motivated, perform track practices, and conduct hill repetitions and recovery runs. This will help to keep the training sessions interesting.

- Plug yourself into a technology gadget when you feel unmotivated to run. The cellphone system can now provide numerous applications that will assist in timing your training, provide tracking of functions, and offer motivational tips on your running. In recent times, there has been an introduction of running watches that have Global Positioning System (GPS) functionalities and can measure key health parameters such as high blood pressure, heartbeat rate, and pulse rate.

- If you load music that excites you, you will be motivated to keep running or increase your running speed by pacing to the tempo of the beat. Music will provide positive emotions and might help bring some past experiences into your mind.

- Running will certainly improve your mental health. Research by nutritionists has proved that running assists in releasing stress, improving your sleep, and calming the mind, thereby reducing depression. A relaxed mind can influence you to keep the habit of running.

- When you envision success in achieving your goal, you are motivated to continue with running. If you start imagining a fitter you and visualizing yourself enjoying your favorite meal because you can longer limit what you take, you will be driven to keep pushing.

- Allocating time to yourself for training is a good way to focus on yourself. You will be driven by the opportunity to meditate, conduct brainstorming sessions on your own, and allow time to reflect on family, dreams, goals, etc.

- Running can provide the opportunity to participate in community work. A good number of races that you might enter are fundraising events for charity work.

- You may be motivated by internal enjoyment and pride. If it is, allow your ego to push you into training and enrolling in races. It is these intrinsic values that can motivate you to stay longer on the course and sustain your training program. You must leverage your pride; this could be the only positive benefit of pride.

- You may run for personal recognition and to uplift your self-esteem. If your ego is stoked when people congratulate you for completing a race, you will be motivated to run.

- When you run in intense programs like training and racing in a marathon, you will lose weight and you are likely to improve your physical appearance. Running will assist in losing weight, toning the body, and shaping the physique. The other health benefits that come with reduced body weight are lessening diabetes complications and heart conditions. Running can improve the flow of blood and oxygen, thus increasing the efficiency of metabolism.

- You might need an inspired push from a professional trainer who is able to drive you to go beyond your limits. When you break the routine, a coach will guide you back. Because your training is being guided by an expert in running, you are likely to train together with professional runners who will rub a positive attitude and passion in you.

- Running has to be enjoyable; it is not supposed to be a job. Make the marathon fun and ignite the training sessions by discovering new areas, integrating new games as a combo with running, and splashing paint in a color run.

- Training for a marathon offers a very good opportunity to train the body. Training programs for a marathon usually take up to six months, allowing you plenty of time to expose your body to exercise.

- The intensity of marathon training will guarantee you a loss in weight. Your desire to look good will motivate you to run.

- Running is a good way of coping with psychological issues.

- If you value your body, running will offer you the opportunity to round your body. Running will also allow you to eat well, drink lots of fluids, eat healthily, and take a good, long sleep. Most runners usually abandon smoking when they start to seriously train for a race.

The Various Techniques of Running

The 'foot strike' is a term that refers to how a person lands their foot every time they lift their leg. The foot strike will affect the speed of the runner, their energy use, and their risk of being injured. Every marathoner will have their own strike pattern, varying because of the height, mass, and structure of the bone.

The five different techniques of running a marathon are discussed below.

1.   Rearfoot Strike

The technique used by most runners is the rearfoot strike, also referred to as the heel strike. With this running method, the heel hits the ground at the back of the foot. The heel strike can be beneficial for turning on sharp curves and also as a breaking tool when reducing speed.

The advantages of landing on the heel are:

- An efficient metabolic rate.

- Offers less pressure to the body with relation to oxygen intake and energy output.

2. Midfoot Strike

The foot center hits the pavement and then distributes the impact evenly across the foot and the entire body. The body weight balances on the hips, knees, and ankles, and allows you to sustain a high and consistent speed that can beat other athletes.

The technique offers a higher probability of attaining high running speeds and also fewer variations in speed. One major setback of the technique is that the athlete will be more open to injuries to the Achilles tendon and the ankle.

3. Forefoot Strike

The toe and the ball of the foot fall on the impact of the ground first, and the heels seldom hit the ground. The upper body is usually bent forward in this strike mode, and cramps are frequent on the calf and the tendon on the Achilles.

This technique is important when powering up a hill or during a sprint toward the finishing line. Forefoot strike has a number of benefits to the athlete, such as:

- The impact on joints is lower compared to other techniques.

- The chances of injury to the knees are less.

- It aids efficiency in the marathon.

- The drawback of this technique is the high likelihood of cramps in the calves and around the tendon in the Achilles.

4. Natural or Barefoot Strike

The technique uses bare feet to run. The foot strike of the natural technique moves from the heel to the mid or forefoot strike. The length of the stride will decrease as you move forward, creating a higher step count and lessening work on the body. The negative forces from the ground will decrease as the count of steps decreases.

This technique is regarded as the most effective form of running, as it is economical and more efficient than the other forms. The natural strike supports the body, and its many benefits have made the technique more fashionable and trendy. Listed below are numerous advantages derived from the technique:

- The muscles of the feet are strengthened because of the natural alignment created by the mother of nature.

- The toes are strengthened. Developing toes assists in maintaining posture.

- Assists in reducing the risk of injury to the knees and ankles because you control your running better and your run is stable.

- Helps in connecting the mind to the body because the feet carry the sensory nerves that input messages to the brain. This improves communication within the entire body.

- Assists in shaping and strengthening the arc on the foot.

- Improves the feedback from the nerves on the forces working on the body and the nature of positioning of the body.

- Reduces the impact on the joints.

- Prevents toes from squishing, thereby reducing challenges like bunions and hammertoe.

- Aids the athlete to run faster.

- Assists the runner to move freely without pain.

- Lowers pain in the back.

The negative side is that the natural form of running exposes the athlete to cuts from the road and may tear off foot muscles due forces from the ground.

5. Chi Running

This form of running borrows its technique from a Chinese boxing art called *t'ai chi*. Chi form of running focuses on the following principles:

- Alignment and walking properly.

- Relaxed legs.

- Core strength.

- Mindfulness.

The technique's outline is channeled towards focusing on the mind, feeling the body as you run, breathing so that you tap into *chi*, relaxing the muscles, and practicing good posturing and a measured start. Athletes are asked to maintain a straight back, a bit leaned forward, with their knees bending a little. The midfoot lands on the pavement and propels you using momentum.

The following are the advantages of Chi running:

- It helps strengthen the core muscles.

- It assists in fusing the mind and the body.

- The focus is on the long-term enhancement of overall health and performance of the athlete.

- It helps in lowering shin splint and IT Band Syndrome, also known the 'iliotibial band condition', which is a state where the tendon gets swollen.

Finding the Correct Technique Suitable for You

The running techniques discussed above will be dependent on the athlete. There are runners who will leverage all the techniques in order to attain an optimum speed on the track. Some athletes select a striking form based on the terrain or the speed they want to run at. The starting point to selecting the foot strike that best suits you are to refine the technique you perform consistently. You are likely to be exposed to injuries when you adopt a new technique. A slight variation of the foot strike might take you out of the cycle and leave you unprotected. A suitable technique for you is one that fits into your natural way of running and allows you to avoid errors. At the top end, the mistakes can make your running less competent. In the extreme end, you could get injured from the mistakes.

Assessing the efficiency of the athlete's stride is always important, whether they are running an Olympic marathon or they are jogging for fun. Athletes are advised to maintain a suitable running technique to improve their efficiency and also avoid injury. With that said, the following tips will assist you in selecting the correct technique.

- You need to avoid over-striding the foot. Regardless of your technique, the spot of contact relative to the body will determine the weight of the impact and the subsequent force needed to stop. In terms of overstriding, you need to watch the alignment of your knee to the position of contact at the initial contact. The knee has to flex directly over the initial contact of the foot. If the athlete is over-striding the ankle will stick ahead. Overstriding could result in poor posture and a slower stride frequency at the targeted speed.

- Maintain a tall posture as you run. Maintaining a tall posture when running is recommended, especially in order to avoid injury. You are advised to maintain a tall posture rather than flexing forward or backward when running. The torso (the trunk of the body) should be straight. The posture you take when you go around your daily chores is likely to spill over into your running because it has become standard to you. Your usual posture will help in reducing tension in your body.

- Ensure your shoulders are relaxed. Maintain your shoulders in a relaxed state when running. Maintaining shoulders in a relaxed mode is key to avoiding inhibiting your arm movements. Your arms provide balance to the body, rhythm, and the power to run. Just as with the legs, the size of your arm movements controls your speed. If the size of the arm movement is longer, then the speed will increase, and vice versa if the movement is smaller.

- Strengthen your buttocks area and the body core muscles. Gluteal muscles, also known as glutes, consist of the gluteus maximus, gluteus medius, and gluteus minimus buttock muscles. The common name for these is 'buttocks'. The group of muscles provides stability around the hips, pelvis, and lower trunk of your body. This stability is necessary, as it influences running performance and the ability to stay injury-free.

- Avoid bouncing and rotating disproportionately. You need to run in movements that are linear as you pace forward. Rotating excessively will counter the overall objective of progressing forward, and you will be using energy inefficiently.

- It is necessary to control breathing. Your overall breathing tempo must align with the rhythm the body is running at. Achieving the correct alignment is fundamental to your running technique and should be trained so that you can be able to sustain composure as you run.

- Remember the running technique is an individual's choice. There has been a lot of discourse around the running techniques, however, it is important to note that there is no scientific evidence that supports one particular form.

Chapter 3:

Building a Tough Mindset

Chapter outline

- Ways to manage mental barriers

- Methods to strengthen your mind

- Adapting yourself to a growth mindset

- Embracing pain

Overcoming Mental Obstacles

Defining Mental Strength

Jaeshke A et al (2020) et al, defines mental strength as the capacity to endure the challenges that a runner faces as they negotiate the marathon course. In addition to that, a mentally tough marathoner is a consistent athlete; one with better determination compared to others, who is focused, confident, and has more control when faced with pressure. Many athletes spend the bulk of their time working on the body to improve endurance, but they often neglect training their mental strength. While most professional runners classify running as 90% mental, the moment the runner gets a block in the mind, there are a number of obstacles that may be difficult to overcome.

The Key is Self-Belief

The key to the achievement of tasks is self-belief. Samantha Gash, an ultra-endurance runner from Australia once said, *"I think I can do anything. If I really want to do it—I think that is the caveat."* Samantha Gash once ran 235 miles without stopping across the Simpson Desert in her home country. Because her mind was determined to run across a desert, Samantha achieved a feat that very few men will accomplish in their lives. If the mind conceives something, then you need to believe it is achievable.

On the day of the race, the mind has birthed a marathon, and working towards the goal should now take over. At the line where the marathon starts, you will need to have a belief that you possess the abilities to accomplish your goal. Preparing the mind to believe is easy these days because the information is readily available, on the internet, to assist in aligning the effectiveness of the mind-to-body connection. As you train for physical fitness, conditioning the mind for success is also equally important.

Planning their mindset by creating images of the marathon course will assist the runner in squeezing an extra 0ne to two percent on the day of the race. The mental imagery will be practiced extensively in the mind to include every possible situation in the upcoming race and every possible undulation on the course. This will make it possible for the runner to leverage confidence levels and a prepared mind. Practicing visualization techniques should roughly take 10 to 15 minutes a day.

Attention to detail and focus on the specifics are necessary when creating images of the race. Picture yourself being surrounded at the starting point, and you hear the sound of the gun. Envisage the pounding of the heart, the fear of being confined when the stampeding starts. When you can invoke these emotions and the images of the surroundings, you are likely to stay calm and perform well in the chaos that comes with starting a marathon.

Prepare an image of both the positive scenarios and the not-so-good encounters during the race. Creating images will help in instilling confidence to know what action to take when the runner meets the situation. Visualizing will assist in creating a specific plan to handle situations that will arise.

A positive takeaway from visualizing during training is that it offers an opportunity to boost an athlete's confidence. As explained earlier, if a runner has high confidence levels, they are likely to run successfully. When you create images of success in your mind, subconsciously, the brain has a belief that you have the ability to be successful. If you remove guessing from the mind, you may be able to replace it with real solutions that bring confidence and determination.

One way to boost the confidence of an athlete is to practice self-affirmations and talking to oneself as a routine every day. Standing for at least five minutes every evening in the mirror while reciting specific messages will help in training self-affirmations. A mirror will assist in engaging the photoreceptors in the brain to internalize the positive affirmations. Reciting words such as, "I will complete well in the race," will help erase doubt in the mind.

As the marathon day approaches, the runner might get nervous, that could be the time to implement the techniques learned during the visualization training in order to ease the nerves. Start by recollecting the great training sessions that you participated in. Remembering the high tempo you engaged during previous successful races will assist in conjuring up similar emotions of accomplishment.

In training the mental strength for success in the marathon, the focus should be put on the following points:

A. Overcome failure by focusing on the immediate drive for success after failure training.

B. Keep reminding yourself of the set goals and aspirations even when it is challenging the mind and the body.

C. See failure when you encounter it, gather learning points, and create a plan to counter the temporary downfall.

D. Allow the mind to familiarize itself with any changes, distractions, and threats while working under pressure.

E. Pick yourself up after a mistake and recover from it.

F. Acquire the necessary patience and discipline to reach your full potential.

G. Have a belief that you can overcome any barriers along the way.

H. Train the mind to put focus on the processes ahead of the outcomes.

I. Develop the ability to train in an environment that is strenuous.

J. Manage anxiety in situations that exert pressure on the mind.

While a lot will certainly happen during the marathon, take the positive out of any situation. It is important for the runner to never quit a race. As hopeless as the situation can be, you should be able to reframe the goals and redraft your aspirations. The mind possesses the ability to alter any outcome of your marathon into a positive experience.

Success in a marathon is defined as starting a race and progressing to the finishing line. However, when you fail to complete the race, you do not have to regard it as a disaster; consider it a learning experience. Whatever the outcome, prepare the mind to accept the result and to refocus if the outcome was negative.

Ways of Strengthening the Mind

Training the Mind

The potential to successfully complete a 26.2-mile race is highly dependent on the toughness of your mind, confidence, and focus at attaining goals. Therefore, a proper plan is needed for training the mind to be tough. Training the mind and the body as a single system that is connected will assist in clarifying the perception of the effort needed to perform. For example, (Southwick et al., 2013), in discussing the development of resilience of the mind, mentions the following variables as critical variables: Developmental programs, genetic composition, and sociocultural factors. Your confidence levels will increase, and your motivation will improve. The concept of training the mind offers an understanding of the ways to improve running.

Mental Toughening Strategies

You may use a variety of mental strategies in order to handle the physical pain and discomfort brought about due to fatigue. The tips below will assist the athlete in toughening the mind for marathons.

1. If you are a solo-runner, words like, "I will feel better after taking a drink at the water point," can help you to push through the challenges of mental fatigue. Practicing gratitude is a good way to self-talk. Thanking yourself for the ability to run, the capacity to endure the course, and being grateful for the available time.

2. Segmenting the marathon into small parts will make the mind form a perception of a manageable distance. Once you start a new segment, you will need to visualize the start of a race, with a fresh body and a mind focused on completing that part of the race. Creating small physical milestones along the route, like the nearest bus stop, a statue, or running at a certain speed for the next three miles, can instill motivation.

3. Another way to trick the mind is to convert mile goals into time goals or vice versa. Your mind might say, "The statue of liberty is only 20 minutes away," when it is two miles away.

4. A marathon is not an easy task, and you will need to internalize the difficulties that come with training for the race and remind yourself that not everyone will be brave enough to participate. This will make the success a worthwhile accomplishment and will lift your emotions.

5. Your mind should recite a slogan while you are racing. This will help you to remain focused on the race and will fire your inner motivation. An example of a catchy slogan is. "Run, sweat, and complete the race."

6. If you create images of a successful run before the marathon, you will tune into those celebratory scenes when you hit a rough patch.

7. Choosing a favorite regalia or something that is close to your heart is useful in helping the mind concentrate on the race. Pick a specific color of clothing, a dog, or a type of vehicle to count as you run through the racecourse. This will keep your mind busy and distracted from the hurt that your body feels.

8. When you develop plans for after the marathon, it will help in making the marathon a secondary target that you need to dispense with quickly before you embark on future plans. Pondering

on what to do after finishing the race assists in organizing your day by allowing you to look ahead to a planned event after the race.

9. Visualize the entire marathon preparation up to the end of the race day. Create images of yourself crossing the finishing line with people cheering you on and posing for photos with friends or officials.

10. The use of a podcast and headphones can assist you with focusing. You can stay focused even with distractions by listening to a podcast at warmup.

11. Practicing a proper breathing technique is useful for sustaining a long run. Elsewhere in this book there is a section that explains the breathing processes.

12. You are encouraged to break the monotony by alternating activities. Always change routes to avoid boredom and monotony and discover new areas by taking detours.

Adjusting Marathon Runners to Adapt a Growth Mindset

The Difference Between a Fixed Mindset and a Growth Mindset

Psychologists make a distinction between a fixed mindset and a growth mindset. A growth mindset believes that any skill can be learned, adapted, or built upon. This mindset gives you confidence that you can develop skills and this gives you the belief that your running performance can be improved. With this belief, you are willing to face the challenges and bear the risks that come with running marathons.

If you possess a growth mindset, you will perceive a rigorous workout or a tough long run as an opportunity to realize your potential. The challenges will make you run faster, grow stronger, and adapt quickly to life situations. Within this mindset, you may be able to assess the results that come with applying effort. A setback or a criticism is viewed as an opportunity to improve and a chance to learn lessons.

- Fixed Mindset

A fixed mindset usually gives athletes the negative opportunity to compare with others. The comparison could lead to rigid athletes that are fearful to take the challenge, which will limit their potential to succeed in running. Overthinking could create a lack of faith in our capabilities to perform well in a marathon, leading to inactivity and a lack of motivation to continue the training.

- Growth Mindset

A lot of research has been conducted on kids in classrooms. The difference between the growth mindset and the fixed mindset, as it relates to running, has been found to be the distance. The psyche and perception of the runner on the distance will determine whether the individual will view the sport as one you can develop or not. In addition to applying more energy in overcoming the test, a growth attitude will value at the prospect to develop critical thinking skills

How to Foster a Growth Mindset in Long-Distance Runners

We have all pondered the following rhetorical questions, especially in situations that are challenging and require extra physical effort:

- Am I good enough?

- Have I trained enough for this marathon?

- Do I belong in a marathon?

- Is my time good enough?

- Was my training program adequate for this race?

Regrettably, almost all runners will question the idea of belonging to a marathon. The words below have probably rung in your mind occasionally after a race:

"I had a poor attitude yesterday, and therefore, ran a crappy race. When I look at my pace and realize how slow I was, I just get demotivated. I am pushing myself beyond my limits. How can I exert more, and how do my running mates find that competitive edge to push to the limit? Let me see if I can pace a little bit more and proceed to run out of my comfort zone. This comfort zone could be my biggest challenge. If I overcome it, I will reward myself with a trip to Honolulu."

Your perception of everything will determine the type of mind that you have. A lot of people see value in confronting challenges because they view that as an opportunity to grow.

In order to adopt a growth mindset, you will need to:

- Learn from your mistakes. Allow your peers or experienced runners to assess your marathon and listen to the negative feedback.

- Accommodate any setbacks along the way because you are going to face a lot of them.

- Begin their practice program by starting slow. Engage in short runs in training and plan the training program around cycles. Take it easy early on as you gradually get into the groove of running.

- Pay attention to the easier tasks that you are able to complete with less effort, especially if they push you to become a better runner.

- Reserve sprinting and running fast for race day.

- Your training intensity should dictate the amount of effort you put in.

Learning to Embrace Pain When Running a Marathon

There is a quote preferred by runners that was made by the legendary Scott Jurek (classified as a living legend, he is an ultramarathoner from Minnesota USA), a legendary ultra-marathoner. The saying goes like this: "Pain only hurts." Runners translate the quote to mean that while pushing and running beyond your limits is certainly uncomfortable, it will not harm your body. At the extreme end of the intensity, you will feel like you are dying, but you are certainly not failing. Professional athletes have a much higher level of tolerance for discomfort than recreational athletes. Runners who sustain through the pain-only-hurts phase subsequently extract the most from their body fitness.

When you soldier through the pain barrier, you are acknowledging that pain is an unavoidable part of the marathon experience. Accommodating the discomfort does not reduce it, but it makes you run through with a lesser perceived effort,

Bracing and detachment are methods used by athletes in order to embrace the pain that comes from running a marathon. Restraining your mind actively from the pain of running is referred to as 'braces'. Detachment involves the separation of your emotions and thoughts from the perceptions to the extent that emotions don't control perceptions. It might be easier for you to control emotion by selecting a preferred state of emotion before it begins. Anger is an emotional state that can enhance performance in running. You might choose this emotionally and therefore, block any other state to come.

Chapter 4:

Building Physical Stamina

Chapter summary

- Difference between 'endurance' and 'stamina'

- Tapering

- Synchronizing pace and breathing

- How to adapt to running a marathon if you suffer from asthma

Defining Stamina

Running long distances assists the body in developing muscles. The science behind running consists of the repeated and sustained movements of legs and arms for long periods. This involves the complex movement of muscles. A weak network of muscles will not last for long periods of time. It is, therefore, important for an athlete to focus on strengthening their stamina. Stamina assists the mind and the body in keeping up with the intensity.

The Difference Between 'Endurance' and 'Stamina'

'Stamina' refers to the strength and energy to sustain a long run such as a marathon. The terms 'stamina' and 'endurance' can both be used with reference to sustained physical activities. The two words may be interchangeably used, however, they are not exactly synonyms. 'Stamina' is used with reference to performance at maximum capacity. Therefore, it stands for both the burden on the body and the mental load of running.

Endurance is a function of performance over a sustained period of time. Endurance measures the resolve and durability of the heart, referred to as 'cardiovascular efficiency'. It basically measures how the heart, lungs, and muscles function collectively to sustain the body by distributing oxygen and blood. The cardiovascular system must be efficient in moving the blood to all the muscles that will be working so that they keep functioning. The objective of endurance in running is to maintain the ability to persist with intense activity.

Rate of Oxygen Intake and Exercise Intensity

The rate of intake of oxygen is measured by a parameter known as VO2. The maximum rate is represented by VO2 max. A measure of VO2 max indicates a quantitative figure that measures endurance fitness training effects in different people. A higher maximum oxygen (VO2 max) intake by an athlete indicates that the heart has an increased ability to endure training exercises. To allow you to relate your measure to elite distance runners, the measure of these athletes is roughly a high of 90mL/ (kg.min). The sport alternates from bursts of intense exercise and a recovery period that require a high intake of oxygen.

Methods of Building Endurance

The following points summarize what you need to pursue in order to build your endurance:

- Increase your training time gradually. This could mean over each week, over the month, or even over the year.

- Raise the running miles by 10% each week, focusing on improving your endurance each week and every month.

- Build the endurance of your muscles by pumping lighter weights and increasing the repetitions every week.

- Within your health limits, of course, do not permit mental or physical blocks to stop you from training.

- Allow time for muscle recovery and mental rejuvenation.

- Hydrate the body and eat carbohydrates to fuel the body.

Consistency is key to building endurance and stamina. The two aspects are built by consistently running as regularly as possible. You will need to draw up a schedule that will dedicate three to four days of running a week. Increase the actual number of runs to gain fitness and experience. If you are a starter in running a marathon, begin by running lower distances per week and gradually increase as you approach race day.

The following are tips to use in order to stick to the plan:

- Set the time on the alarm: Allow an alarm to remind you of your marathon goals. An alarm can also be used as a cue to direct you to a workout.

- Get a partner to run with: Adherence to a workout plan can improve if you have a friend that you are running with. A combination of social time and physical activity can be a perfect match for the road.

- Plan the workout in advance: Scheduling runs will assist you in getting around busy periods.

Ways to Build Stamina and Endurance

If you want to be a marathoner, you will need to consider performing the following in order to improve your stamina. Most runners pay particular attention to the important aspects of speed during training, strength, and endurance. Stamina is, however, unappreciated, yet it combines various fitness components. You will need to accommodate the following methods in order to build your stamina.

- Gradually increase the mileage as you progress with your training schedule. Marathoners generally rely on a 10 percent rule in athletics. The rule outlines that if you want to be effective, you will need to increase your practice mileage by a minimum of 10 percent every week. This gives the body time to adjust to the increases in load and also aids in preventing injuries.

- Include High-Intensity Interval Training (HIIT) in the training plan. HIIT is a training regime that is used to boost endurance. Interval training may involve a workout on a steep slope. A 30-second run up the slope can be followed by a 60-second walk down the hill. HIIT trains the heart and lungs to cope with long periods of running. Running at high intensity allows the muscles to handle lactic acid (a by-product of respiration) in a more efficient way and, therefore, avoid feeling burning sensations.

- Rehearse on explosive exercises (Plyometrics). Explosive training, like squat jumps and jumping jacks, exerts a full force in a short

HIIT/ Plyometrics

space of time. The maximum force from this explosive exercise increases muscle power.

- Building stamina is assisted in the following ways:

    ○ Increases the capacity to reserve energy in between muscle movements. The energy can then be transferred into increasing body speed, as the body can now produce a force with more efficiency.

    ○ Strengthens your muscles. When you work against resistance, it exposes your muscles to new stresses which trigger muscle expansion and also make the muscles stronger.

    ○ Promotes flexibility of the muscles.

- Stamina handles emotional stress and stress to the body exceptionally well. Stress has the negative effect of compromising your body. The immune system will drop, as there will be an imbalance in the production of hormones caused by a sharp increase in adrenaline and cortisol. Your sleep becomes sporadic, and all other processes might go on pause. It can help to manage stress by meditating, practicing yoga, and performing aerobics.

- Run in intervals of 800 yards. Endurance is improved by incorporating small bursts of 800 yards in the training plan. Running a number of sprints that are interspersed will assist in improving performance. This method of training can help in stimulating energy in the long run.

- Include strength training in the training regime. Whether you are a beginner or an experienced athlete, strength training is needed to improve performance. It will help in the economic use of oxygen and, therefore, maintain a longer pace. The strength training regime can incorporate the exercises below:

  o Deadlifts

  o Squats

  o Overhead weightlifting

  o Leg and arm lunges

  o Bent over row

- The motion of running is repetitive. You persist in hitting the ground while moving forward and swinging your arms. The repetitions can be monotonous, and it would be good to vary your activities. If you alternate running with activities such as yoga, aerobics training, dancing, and strength training, you will break the monotony. Cross-training can offer runners an opportunity to build strength while avoiding over-running. You can use cross-training to target various body angles that you need to build extensively in order to improve your running. You could join group training classes that target core muscles and the upper body because these areas are neglected when running. With technology these days, you might not need to leave the house since virtual classes are conducted either on television or on the internet.

- Drink coffee or a caffeinated drink before you train. Drinking a cup of heavy coffee or a caffeinated drink will assist in increasing your energy levels, your attitude during training, and your physical capabilities. The reservation is that caffeine can be addictive and needs to be taken in limited quantities.

Tapering in Marathon Training

According to Smythe B and Lawlor A (2021), 'taper' refers to the period when athletes reduce their load during the weeks before the race day. Tapering assists runners with recovery from the pressures of sustained training at high intensity. The aim of the recovery period is to enhance performance during race day.

Defining the Taper

A lot of recreational marathon runners will not pursue a disciplined training program. The taper period is defined as the reduction of intensity in training as the athlete approaches race day. The taper period is approximately four weeks before the marathon day. Professional athletes, who are more competitive, will follow a more controlled taper that involves gradually reducing the levels of training some weeks prior to race day. The approach to tapering by recreational marathoners is usually not as structured. The baseline or the days of intense activity are the weeks preceding the start of the taper period.

An Example of a Taper Program

A marathoner running an average of, say, 23 miles five to six weeks prior to the taper period might reduce the distance covered to an average of 20 miles in the four to three weeks before the race. Progressively, the distances are reduced by about 30%, week on week, until a few days before the race.

Tabulated below is an example of a tapering program that takes into account the level running that you have developed:

Level	Total Miles During Training	Tapering Time	Percentage Decrease in Milage	Taper Mileage Average
Beginner	about 30 miles per week	three to four weeks	25 to 35%	20 miles/week
Intermediate	about 40 miles per week	three to two weeks	15% to 25%	30 to 35 miles/week
Professional	about 50 miles per week	one to two weeks	10% to 15%	45 miles/week

Some Recovery Tips that are Doable During the Tapering Period

When you slow down in training, you may occupy the extra time with flexibility work, drills to avoid injury, relaxed paced-up running, and preparing race day logistics. This will assist in maintaining the momentum picked up during intense training. The following recovery tips are recommended:

- Rolling to overcome IT Band Syndrome and injury to the knee. You may perform this exercise using a foam rubber roll, a tennis ball, or a golf ball. Perform this exercise till the day of the race.

- Immerse yourself in an ice bath for a maximum of 15 minutes for a period of two to three times a week to enable your blood vessels to contract. This method has the added advantages of aiding the reconstruction of broken tissues and also assists in reducing inflammation.

- Perform salt baths to increase the flow of blood. Do this exercise at least two to three times weekly.

- Drinking hydration shots, mineral salts, and taking vitamin IV tablets will ensure your body is fully hydrated.

- Ensure a good and deep slumber almost every day of the taper period. This should be the period of some of your best sleep.

Adjusting Pace and Synchronizing Breathing

When you are running, synchronizing your breath is important because you rely on your breath to improve your running performance to the maximum. As you continue to train, adjust your breathing so that you find the optimum breathing cycle that allows you to run up to your highest pace. At the start, new pacing speeds might be uncomfortable or painful, but as you continue to flow with new speeds, you will enjoy adapting to the new optimum breath suitable for your running.

Why is Breathing Difficult When You are Running?

Running is an intense sport that causes the respiratory system and the body to work beyond their daily limits. At that level of activity, you require a lot of oxygen to sustain your breath and purge the carbon dioxide. The response of your breathing to the intensity of your pacing can be a pointer to your level of fitness. You should not struggle to breathe, both while training and while running. If you run beyond your capability, you will either fall short of breath or start to wheeze in the chest.

Breathe Through the Nose or Mouth?

The techniques discussed below will assist you in improving your performance. If you practice one technique within one week of your training routine, it can help you identify the best method for you. Research has shown that breathing through the mouth is more efficient compared to using the nose. You will also converse easily when you breathe through the mouth even at high-intensity. When you inhale or exhale using the mouth, a lot more oxygen enters your body to give fuel to the muscles. In addition, breathing through the mouth assists in relieving congestion. Avoid running in congested environments so that you have access to fresh air.

Inhaling and exhaling through your mouth allows more oxygen to enter your body and fuel your muscles. Plus, mouth breathing helps to relieve tension and tightness in your jaw, which can help you to relax your face and body. Consider the following guidelines for breathing while you are running:

- Breathing through the diaphragm. Breathing deeply using the abdomen will toughen the muscles that sustain your breathing allowing you to breathe more air. The following sequence is how you should go about when you practice diaphragmatic breathing:

    1. Lie on your belly and get the sensation for belly breathing.

    2. Fill your belly through your nose.

    3. As the stomach is expanding, it pushes your diaphragm down and out.

    4. Structure your breathing such that your exhaling is longer than when you inhale.

- Perform five training sessions of breathing composed of five minutes each for about five days so that you gain confidence with the technique. When you are confident with your breathing, slowly integrate it into your running.

- Pay particular attention to your breathing. It will allow you to enhance the function and capacity of the lungs as you develop breath awareness.

- When you need to maximize your breath, position your body so that your head is in line to the spine. Avoid leaning forward or backward.

- Create a breathing rhythm. In order to avoid muscular imbalances, you will need to alternate your exhaling with your right or left foot. When you create a rhythm in your breathing, you exert less pressure on the diaphragm and, therefore, spread the impact to both sides of the body.

- Ensure you inhale fresh air by avoiding congested places and areas where there are a lot of fumes from vehicles.

Recommended Tips for Asthmatic People

It is always advised to consult your doctor when you enter an exercise program and you are asthmatic, have a chronic obstructive respiratory disease, or suffer from pulmonary emphysema and/or chronic bronchitis. People with asthma are advised to stay active, even if doing so heightens their symptoms. If you follow the correct approach, your lung function can improve, enhancing the chances of managing the symptoms better. Below are breathing tips for asthmatic runners:

1. Assess the weather before you take to the road. When you run in cold air, use a scarf to cover the air so that you can moisten and inhale warm air. Try running indoors if the weather is ruthless.

2. Perform a warm-up exercise to allow more air into your lungs. Slowly ease into the intense part of training. Allow your lungs to progressively cool down.

3. Avoid running in pollen or wear a pollen mask. Ensure you understand the pollen content outside by checking the pollen count on weather programs before running outdoors.

4. The following breathing techniques are recommended for asthmatic people to improve their breathing and sustain the running:

    -   nasal breathing

    -   the Papworth method

    -   Buteyko breathing

    -   deep yogic breathing

The bottom line is, with the right tools, you can improve your breathing patterns while you run. These straightforward techniques can help you to breathe and run at your full potential. Aim to run at a pace that allows you to breathe easily and carry on a normal conversation without struggling to breathe.

Get in the habit of tuning into your breath not only as you run, but at various times throughout the day. Remind yourself to maintain a smooth, even breath, and pay attention to any variations as well as how your breath responds to certain situations or activities.

Chapter 5:

Motivation: How to Keep

Engaged

Chapter overview

- Willpower to stay engaged

- Preparing for a marathon

- Staying engaged

- Maintaining the enthusiasm

- Benefits of joining an athletics club

How You Stay Motivated to Complete the Program

Training for a marathon could easily be one the most challenging tasks that push your determination to withstand the training to the limit. The willpower to remain connected to the task is needed because you can easily retire to the lounge to sit and watch movies. To stay engaged throughout the set schedule, you will need to keep the inspiration, maintain the enthusiasm, and stay motivated.

Once you set your eyes on successfully completing a marathon, practices need to commence at least six months before the race. By preparing at least six months in advance, you allow yourself adequate time to practice and get into that habit of running. It also gives you plenty of time to stay engaged in the processes. If you are a beginner, start running from one mile until you build up to at least 20 miles.

IMPT

Joining an athletics club is a good motivator in itself. It demonstrates a commitment to achieving your running goals. It assists you in connecting with people of similar interests and creating social groups. A running club will provide suitable facilities for training as well. When you join a club for running, it is a serious step of intent and will assist you in improving your skills for running.

If you join a running club, it gives you a psychological boost to refer to yourself as a runner. Here are some benefits of joining:

1. Offers an opportunity to create friends with likeminded people. You may then be able to partner with a few people who can follow the same training program. It can be very helpful, especially for women who favor safety and protection.

2. You get pushed to run faster by running with others. Your competitive edge can be boosted

Joining an athletics club

by others, which can result in improved performance.

3. You will use the club as a source of running information such as the nearest physiotherapist, off road routes, prices of running gear, and other relevant info.

4. You will have access to professional coaching guidance.

5. Pick inspiration from experienced people. When you join a club, you surround yourself with athletes that have experience and people who are enthusiastic. Rather than depending on your individual motivation, you are likely to be inspired by others in the long term. Experienced people in the club will know how to handle a novice, and they can inspire you to do greater by shortening your learning curve.

cool Title

6. Joining a club will assist in achieving consistency in training. The best method to become a reliable runner is to train consistently. A regular training session broken down into a daily program, a weekly schedule, and a monthly plan will assist you in sticking to a training session. Training in a group and adhering to a program of training off-season is necessary if you want to achieve consistency

7. Reach a level of accountability. A social group, such as your mates at the same club, can hold you accountable when you feel the urge to retire early in the training session or the race. If your

mates are relying on you to lead them during a session, you are more motivated to run.

8. Improvement through social facilitation. The term 'social facilitation' refers to improving your performance through the presence of other participants. Psychologists have proven that if you run in a group, you are likely to adjust to the pace of the group subconsciously. Your brain is pushing you to align to the pace around you.

9. Acquire new acquaintances. You are likely to meet people with the same passion as you; a passion for exercise through running. The relationships formed can become lifelong and will motivate you to train and run in many marathons.

10. Lessons learned from running mates. Running in groups can be a great tactic that allows you to pick some tips that might make you a better athlete.

11. A lot of the clubs will use coaching clinics, literature on running, and other tools necessary to make you a better runner. If you stick to the group long enough, you get some experiences rubbing off from more knowledgeable marathoners.

12. You are safer running in a group than on your own. If you run in a group of athletes, you are more noticeable to car drivers, and this will help in avoiding accidents. You are safer in a group

than running alone because the next runner can help if you need assistance when you are either injured or you feel sick during a race.

Creating a training plan for yourself is a good motivator. Drafting a training schedule helps in creating a path to succeed in running a marathon. When there is no plan, the training is random and not structured. A training plan helps you avoid excuses when you are not motivated to train. You can always tell yourself to stick to the plan.

By registering to participate in marathons, you are creating a bigger goal to target. Signing up and participating in shorter marathons as you gear yourself to successfully run a marathon keeps you engaged in the training program. Start by running five miles for some time, upscale to 10 miles, and proceed until you are ready to run a marathon consistently.

Running in marathons can provide an opportunity to run for a generous cause. When you run for charity, you raise money and channel the proceeds to the needy people of society. Running for charitable organizations can help in motivating you for training. The thought of giving to a worthy cause can help arouse positive emotions in you.

Letting your peers know you are running in a marathon is a tip that is designed to let your social circles check on you. Peer reviews of performance is regarded as one of the measures that can fuel success in sports. The social pressures from your friends can force you to succeed. Your friends will likely refer to you as a legitimate runner, and this can help boost your

yes!

drafting my
training plan

confidence. It is highly likely that when friends are checking, you will not abandon the plan.

A marathon is an opportunity to socialize. Running sessions will be easier if you treat marathons as opportunities to socialize with new acquaintances and expand your business network. You can use social media to your advantage by linking your training program to Instagram or Facebook as running accounts. This will allow you to join running groups, opening the opportunities to follow friends, and join other marathon communities. Messages posted on the groups can put fire under your feet and motivate you to go further. Social media used in this way can also act as a peer review mechanism.

Running can avail the chance to run together with friends. You can get a boost by running with friends. The company will bring social accountability and motivation, as friends you can help cheer each other and lift one another in times when one feels discouraged.

Get your environment ready for running. Attending all household chores in time helps in orienting the mind towards going to a marathon. Try making the processes leading to a marathon as seamless as possible by preparing all the running gear, water, and car keys. You will need to prioritize your plans for activities before a marathon, so that you are primed and motivated to go.

Cut the excuses from your life. There are times when it is necessary to focus on the big picture and remove the crap that might get your head down. Cutting the excuses and putting extra effort on actions around the

Build a social media running account on instagram

set goals will allow you to stay engaged and prepare you for success.

Create a combo of workouts. Running a marathon can be monotonous, and creating a combination of exercises will break the depressing sequence. A combo of training types will break the boredom and introduce some excitement in your training. You could change practice locations, alter the training routine, and include speed bursts in the program.

Tune in to something engaging. Put on your headphones and listen to stuff that will interest you. It could be audio books, music, or podcasts.

Engage in mindful running. If you are alert to everything that is happening all the time, it can remove boredom, give you a sense of focus, and improve motivation.

Reward yourself for progress. Celebrate a successful run by acknowledging your progress. When you reward yourself after completing a marathon, you can restore your motivation in times that you want to retire. The brain will respond by producing a hormone called 'dopamine' that creates excitement in your body. This hormone stores clarity of the mind and assists in releasing stress.

Chapter 6:

How to Train With a

Purpose For a Marathon

Chapter overview

- Primary goal of running a marathon

- Points to consider when setting marathon goals

- Categories of marathon goals

- Alignment of running goals

For most athletes, running a marathon is a personal challenge. The challenges could include losing weight, attaining a healthier life, setting time limits for yourself, and raising awareness for charitable organizations. Keep the reasons in mind because when the body gets tired or the weather turns rough during the race, sustained motivation will get you to succeed in achieving the reasons you picked a marathon in the first place.

Sustained motivation

Training to Achieve Your Primary Goal

You will certainly have a top priority goal when you embark on running a marathon. The usual primary goal for running a marathon is to enjoy the race. Running will come with unpredictable variables. In setting a training program with a purpose, you must not allow goals that limit your love for the sport.

Many runners, whether professional or recreational, take to the road because they have a passion for the sport. The aura of the race, with friends and other running mates surrounding you, along with being cheered by multitudes of supporters, creates an unforgettable intrinsic feeling of achievement. The experience at the end of the race, that elation you get at crossing the line, is fantastic and memorable.

Running goals can either be tangible or intangible. The tangible goals will usually be the fringe benefits along the way to realizing the intangible goals. Tangible goals stand as steppingstones that are necessary to achieve intangible goals. Intangible goals have become bigger goals that can help define your participation in a long-lasting sport such as running.

Issues to Consider When You are Setting Goals for Your Marathon

The primary reasons you have selected running a marathon are usually to achieve some consistency in running by having fun while running and avoiding injury. When you win in these primary objectives, you may realize the following secondary objectives that are vital to you as well:

1. Cardiovascular fitness.

2. Control of body weight.

3. Reduction of stress levels.

4. Lowering of hypertension.

5. Lowering of sugar in the blood.

6. Attaining a healthy mind.

Running is generally strenuous and sustaining a consistent level is difficult. When periods of less motivation occur, you will need to align your training plan with both your health circumstances and fun activities. Some runners will settle for long-term objectives while others commit to run three to four times a week for a time as low as 30 minutes per run. Setting your goals for running will help you enjoy the marathon and keep you motivated to run.

Categories of Goals for Running

Process goals: These goals can also be referred to as 'short-term goals' since they act as steppingstones to achieving the longer-term intangible goal of training to a level where you recover fully to run again the next day. The goals could include sleeping well every night, increasing mobility, eating well every meal time, and handling small tasks with ease. Process goals focus on grasping the task of running and training to improve the skill of running. Areas to pay attention to include a packed training plan, working on refining the nutrition plan, studying marathon principles regularly, seeking advice from the coach on a regular basis, and ensuring you rest well.

Listed below are some of the process goals that can help you in reaching the long-term goals of either running a big city marathon or successfully completing a marathon under a set time:

1. Targeting to run a defined number of days per week.

2. Setting aside a minimum total number of miles that you run per month.

3. Ensuring you sleep seven to eight hours every day.

4. Eating nutrition that fuels your running every session.

5. Training with recovery the next day in mind, ensuring that you are energetic enough to keep training.

6. Keeping the running exciting every session.

7. Performing strength training at least three days a week.

8. Performing one session of Yoga training a week.

9. Performing the following drills at least two times a week:

   • A number of strides per week.

   • Mobility stretches.

   • Speed runs or hill climbs.

10. Ensuring proper warming up of the body before training.

11. Identifying and performing cross training sessions each week.

Outcome goals: The group consists of the desired product of running a marathon. They can include successfully completing a big marathon, such as the Boston marathon, attaining a 10% reduction in weight, or similar measurable goals.

Issues to Consider When Setting the Goals

- Timing: Reassess your goals if you relocate to a new city. Otherwise, ensure that the goals that you are targeting align to the possible marathon courses, anticipated ambient conditions, and environment when the race takes place.

- Gather training information: Read books, articles on running, and marathon magazines, attend credible training on running, and search the internet for information on running.

- Enjoy the process: Enjoy the processes of training and running more than attaining your goals.

- Appreciate reaching the destination: When you achieve your goals, take time to treat yourself to some fun. You may enjoy a dinner out with your family.

- Set aside time to train every week: Plan each day so that you are left with enough time to train on the days that you set out to train.

- Plan to train for a longer period: Before you set a goal, make sure you have adequate time to train for success. Assess the time you are running at the moment in considering the practicability of running a marathon. Presently, if you are running an average of three miles in practice, successfully completing a marathon could be impossible. However, if you have two months or more before the race, you will have enough time to adapt to a marathon by increasing the miles you run in training.

- Align your goals to your natural athletic ability: Not everyone will be born with the talent to run a marathon. Assess your natural talent and know your limits to running.

- Own the marathon objectives: Create goals that you own. Don't copy the running objectives of a training partner. While training with a partner is good, stick to your abilities and avoid being emotionally attached to your partner.

- Create short-range objectives that lead to big goals: Reduce your targets to a short horizon of six months or less. Achieving short-term targets will motivate you to adjust to focusing on long-term goals.

- Align the goals into three tiers: Break your objectives into three tiers, for example:

  o Satisfactory goals can be objectives that allow you to complete a race comfortably and without injury.

  o Moderate goals could be to run a race in under four hours.

- Extremely challenging goals will be setting an objective of completing a race in under three and a half hours.

- Create a flexible plan: Target goals that are less ambitious and prepare to lower expectations when the goals become difficult to reach. The plan should include the possibility of cross-training, for example, if you get injured.

- Measure your goals, write them down, and tell your friends: When you tell your friends about the goals you have set, they will appreciate the commitment you have made in running.

The following tips can be helpful to achieve your objectives:

- Select a suitable plan for training: You will need to select a training plan that is appropriate for you. If you are a beginner, a solid schedule will prepare you for the debut. Because information on training is now available at the touch of a button, you can have an easy access training plan that is suitable on the internet.

- Employ time-managing values: The activities leading to a marathon are numerous, and you will need to efficiently manage them all so that you may be able to run effectively. It may be helpful to write down all extra activities outside your work. Include all the activities in your daily planner and allocate time for each task.

Start the Training

The training program should include a warm-up phase and a period when the body will be allowed to cool down.

- Know your limitations: The amount of pressure placed on the body when you run a race of 26.2 miles exposes you to a higher risk of injury. To avoid injury, consulting your physician is necessary before commencing any training program.

- Start training early: Research has shown that consistent marathoners run for a minimum of a year before registering to run a marathon. Injuries to the body are frequent when you build your weekly mileage too soon. You must never underestimate the need to run at least one 20-miler every week in preparation to run a marathon.

- Cross training and aligning activities: Cross training involves choosing to train in a sport that will complement your running. Avoid stop-and-go sports like basketball and squash. Cross training has become an important aspect to athletes as they battle with staying injury-free during their training and avoiding monotony. The strategy involves alternating running with activities such as yoga, aerobics, swimming, and building muscle. When handled properly, cross training can make you a better athlete. When you vary the training activities, you may benefit by:

- ○ Lessening exposure to injury.

- ○ Improving muscle strength and endurance of the heart.

- ○ Improving body strength will improve the efficiency of the body to utilize energy.

- ○ Providing training opportunities for athletes that are injured to the extent that they cannot run.

- ○ Offering an opportunity to break from running.

- ○ Making you a well-rounded athlete.

Selecting the Best Marathon for You

Nowadays, the range of marathons is extensive, from country road races to urban races where spectators line the roads cheering the runners. You may start by volunteering to work on a race or go to a race nearby as a spectator. This will help you to identify race preferences. How you choose the next marathon will depend on a lot of factors. While a home marathon has certain clear advantages, a foreign race can also present positive returns:

- A local race has the advantage of minimizing travel costs, allowing you to sleep in your house, which means sleeping in your own bed and eating regular food.

- When choosing a local race, you are selecting a race course that you are familiar with. You can easily visualize key sites and plan your pacing speed correctly right throughout the entire race course.

- A foreign race presents opportunities to tour. It means visiting a new place and seeing places that have a new outlook and a fresh atmosphere. Destination races may also assist you with focusing on the race with limited distractions.

- Foreign races will, however, mean added stress due to extra planning on logistics, and they may even incur additional expenses.

- A destination race will bring excitement, especially if it is a first marathon because the focus will be more on completing the race rather than setting a time.

The type of support you will choose to attend should be people who encourage you to improve your performances and experience:

- If you invite families and close allies, the race experience will be much sweeter. You will derive more energy that will boost your running when you see them cheering you on.

- Select a race venue that will provide a good vacation for your family and friends; a venue that is easily accessible to spectators and allows them to spectate easily.

- Choose a race course that has proper signages including humorous signs that will make you laugh.

- If you would rather go to a marathon on your own, then just select marathons that are in small towns. Smaller marathons will allow you to focus on your performance.

The Four Blocks of Marathon Training

Any good program to run in a marathon is built on four blocks. These are:

1. Base mileage: Start by running a small mileage of, say, five miles three to four times the first week. Increase the mileage consistently over time until you are able to run a marathon every week.

2. The long run: Gradually practice the longer run every seven to 10 days so that the body can adjust to longer mileages.

3. Speed work: Practice intervals and tempo runs to increase your cardio capacity.

4. Rest and recovery: Adequate rest helps prevent injuries and mental burnout.

First Block: Base Mileage

Develop a training plan that ranges for up to five months before the race. If you are a starter, the target is to increase the mileage to up to 50 miles per week over the five-month period. The frequency of running should not be more than five runs a week. When you carry out these runs, ensure you are relaxed and you are able to carry out a conversation. When building your base mileage, you must not increase your weekly by more than 10 percent week on week.

NOTE

Second Block: The Long Run

The second block is to build up the long run by increasing the weekly training mileage. The strategy should be to extend the long run by a mile or two every week. After three weeks, reduce the distance by a few miles so that the body is not overworked. For instance, the regime could be structured like this; you run 13 miles on one Friday, 14 miles on the next Friday, and 15 the following Friday. The mile will be reduced to 12 on the fourth Friday before scaling up to 15 miles on the fifth Friday.

Running the distance at a slower pace than normal assists the body in learning to burn fat, building confidence, and allowing your body to adapt to running.

IMPT FOR MY weight Loss GOALS

The maximum distance when training is usually a long run of 20 miles. The extra six miles are extracted on race day from the peak shape of the body, adrenaline, and crowd support during the actual marathon race on the day.

wow!

Third Block: Speed Work

A speed work pillar is an option that can be included in the training plan. It will improve the aerobic capacity and lighten the load when running. The most popular runs for speed work are the tempo run and the interval run.

Intervals runs are composed of short bursts of speed that are repeated at regular intervals. In between the speed bursts, you will include small jogs for recovery. An example is a four-mile run at a high pace and a slow jog of five minutes in between the repeats of the mile runs.

Tempo runs consist of runs that are longer than an interval, usually four to 10 miles, which have you running at a sustainable pace. The workout conditions the body and trains the mind to sustain work that is challenging for longer periods.

Fourth Block: Rest and Recovery

Rest is important when you want to safeguard against injury. Resting days will be days when there is no running. The days allow the muscles to recover from demanding training sessions and may assist in preventing mental exhaustion. During recovery days, you could remain active by incorporating cross-training sessions that could include strength training in the gym and swimming.

At least four weeks before the race, you will need to taper off. In tapering, you reduce the total miles you run so that the body rests.

A Day or Two Before the Marathon

The five days prior to a race are crucial because they set the tone for your approach to a marathon. Whether you are a beginner or a marathon veteran, you will have nerves that will trouble you as you approach a race. There will be a few training tips that will assist you in handling the apprehensiveness that comes when you edge toward a marathon. However, the following five tips are recommended for you in the few days and hours before you run a big race.

You are advised to always maintain a positive mindset during your training program. You will need to religiously stick to the training plan. The challenge is that as you edge towards the marathon, you have to reduce the miles that you run, and this creates ample time that can be difficult to channel toward race activities. Psychologists recommend the employment of visualization methods when doubt starts to creep in. This can assist you to remove doubt as you start seeing yourself successfully completing the race. You will feel motivated if you create images of yourself pacing towards the finishing line, looking at the race clocks and the general processes during the race.

The more you create images, including images of how you overcome boredom, tiredness, and fatigue, the more it becomes easier for you to slowly blend into the race.

Prepare for the race. You will need to organize everything necessary on the marathon day. Prepare a checklist that will include gear for running, water for hydration, snacks, your allocated race number, and all other ancillaries that will support your race. The preparations should include travel arrangements if you are racing out of town.

Take time to carb load. The complementary strategy will be decreasing the amount of exercise a few days before the race. Scientists calculate the body's natural reserve lasts for around 90 minutes of intense activity. The time needed to complete a marathon is in excess of two hours. This means in order to successfully complete the race, a runner will need extra glycogen to cover the more than 30 minutes of intense activity. The plan should make you look to eat an extra eight to 10 grams of carbohydrates per kilogram of body weight throughout the day.

Plan to rest for, at most, two days before the race. Because the race is a long 26-mile course, you will need as much energy as you can get. Resting and reserving energy for one or two days before the race will ensure you are loaded to tackle the race. Ensure you get plenty of sleep before the race, but also get the maximum joy you can get.

Stick to your race plans. Plan your route to the starting point with a lot of precision. Stay focused and stick to your race rituals before and after the race.

On race day, it is recommended to pursue a structured plan of activities. This is the suggested plan for a race that begins at 9am.

Time	Activities
0600 hrs. - 0630 hrs.	1. Wake up 2. Bathe 3. Eat breakfast 4. Take in coffee or a caffeinated drink
0630 hrs. - 0730 hrs.	1. Load running gear into the car 2. Drive to race course
0730 hrs. - 0800 hrs.	1. Explore around the race venue 2. Inspect transition zones

	3. Set up your transition area 4. Drink water
0800 hrs. - 0820 hrs.	1. Attend race briefing
0820 hrs. - 0830 hrs.	1. Perform short jogs 2. Conduct stretches
0830 hrs. - 0840 hrs.	1. Wear your wetsuit 2. Wear running shoes
0840 hrs. - 0900 hrs.	1. Warm up 2. Do dynamic stretches 3. Take an energy gel 4. Take hydrating fluids
0900 hrs.	1. Begin race

The runner may then tweak the plan depending on the time of the race.

Typical marathon gear may consist of the following items:

- A running smartwatch,

- Comfortable shoes designed for running,

- A Dri-fit top or a technical running top (a top that dries sweat quickly),

- Sweat absorbing socks,

- A bra that is designed for running,

- Chafe protector,

- Sweat wiping band,

- Running shorts, tights, or pants,

- Hydration equipment,

- Nutrition plan,

- Elastic band designed to facilitate stretching,

- Hydrating fluids,

- Snacks.

Plan your route to the starting point with a lot of precision. Stay focused and stick to your race rituals before and after the race.

Please see below for a training plan to help you structure your journey towards a marathon.

Training Plan to Run a Marathon in Six Months: A Program to Take from the Couch to Active Life

Week/Day	Monday	Tuesday	Wednesday	Thursday	Friday	Saturday	Sunday

Week One	Walk for 15 minutes	Walk for four minutes, then run for one minute (Repeat the above four times)	Walk for 20 minutes	Walk for three and half minutes. Run for one and half minutes (Repeat the above for five times)	Rest day	Walk for three and a half minutes. Run for one and half minutes (Repeat four times) Walk half a minute. Run one	Rest day

							and half min utes (Rep eat thre e time s)	

Week Two	Walk for 15 minutes	Walk for two and half minutes, then run for two and half minutes (Repeat the above five times)	Walk for 25 minutes	Walk for two minutes. Run for three minutes (Repeat the above for five times)	Rest day	Walk two minutes. Run for three minutes (Repeat four times) Walk half a minute. Run two and half minutes	Rest day

						(Repeat two times)	

Week Three	Walk for 30 minutes	Walk for one and a half minutes, then run for three and a half minutes (Repeat the above five times)	Walk for 35 minutes	Walk for one and a half minutes, then Run for three and a half minutes (Repeat the above for six times)	Rest day	Walk one and a half minutes. Run for three and a half minutes (Repeat four times) Walk half a minute. Run	Rest day

							two and a half minutes (Repeat two times)	

Week Four	Walk for 35 minutes	Walk for one minute, then run for four minutes (Repeat the above six times)	Walk for 40 minutes	Walk for half a minute, then run for four and a half minutes (Repeat the above for six times)	Rest day or 30 minutes of Yoga	Walk half a minute. Run for four and a half minutes (Repeat six times) Walk half a minute. Run two and a	Rest day

First Full Mile Run week 5

						half min utes (Rep eat two time s)	
Wee k Five	Cros s Trai ning	Run a dista nce of one mile	Stre ngth exer cise or Aero bics	Run a dista nce of one mile	Rest day or 30 min utes of Yog a	Run for two mile s	Rest day

Week Six	Cross Training	Run a distance of two miles	Strength exercise or aerobics training	Run a distance of two miles	Rest day or 30 minutes of Yoga	Run for three miles	Rest day
Week Seven	Cross Training	Run a distance of three miles	Strength exercise or aerobics training	Run a distance of three miles	Rest day or 30 minutes of Yoga	Run for four miles	Rest day
Week Eight	Cross Training	Run a distance of three miles	Strength exercise or aerobics training	Run a distance of three miles	Rest day or 30 minutes of Yoga	Run for five miles	Rest day

Week Nine	Cross Training	Run a distance of three miles	Strength exercise or aerobics training	Run a distance of three miles	Rest day or 30 minutes of Yoga	Run for four miles	Rest day
Week Ten	Cross Training	Run a distance of four miles	Strength exercise or aerobics training	Run a distance of four miles	Rest day or 30 minutes of Yoga	Run for six miles *10K*	Rest day
Week Eleven	Cross Training	Run a distance of four miles	Strength exercise or aerobics training	Run a distance of four miles	Rest day or 30 minutes of Yoga	Run for seven miles	Rest day
Wee	Cros	Run	Stre	Run	Rest	Run	Rest

k Twel ve	s Trai ning	a dista nce of four mile s	ngth exer cise or aero bics train ing	a dista nce of one mile	day or 30 min utes of Yog a	for five mile s	day
Wee k Thir teen	Cros s Trai ning	Run a dista nce of thre e mile s	Stre ngth exer cise or aero bics train ing	Run a dista nce of one mile	Rest day or thirt y min utes of Yog a	Run for eight mile s	Rest day
Wee k Four teen	Cros s Trai ning	Run a dista nce of thre e mile s	Stre ngth exer cise or aero bics train ing	Run a dista nce of thre e mile s	Rest day or 30 min utes of Yog a	Run for 10 mile s	Rest day

Week Fifteen	Cross Training	Run a distance of five miles	Strength exercise or aerobics training	Run a distance of five miles	Rest day or 30 minutes of Yoga	Run for eight miles	Rest day
Week Sixteen	Cross Training	Run a distance of four miles	Strength exercise or aerobics training	Run a distance of four miles	Rest day or 30 minutes of Yoga	Run for 12 miles	Rest day
Week Seventeen	Cross Training	Run a distance of three miles	Strength exercise or aerobics training	Run a distance of three miles	Rest day or 30 minutes of Yoga	Run for 14 miles	Rest day

Half Marathon

Week Eighteen	Cross Training	Run a distance of three miles	Strength exercise or aerobics training	Run a distance of three miles	Rest day or 30 minutes of Yoga	Run for 10 miles	Rest day
Week Nineteen	Cross Training	Run a distance of four miles	Strength exercise or aerobics training	Run a distance of four miles	Rest day or 30 minutes of Yoga	Run for 16 miles	Rest day
Week Twenty	Cross Training	Run a distance of four miles	Strength exercise or aerobics training	Run a distance of four miles	Rest day or 30 minutes of Yoga	Run for 18 miles	Rest day

Week							
Week Twenty-One	Cross Training	Run a distance of four miles	Strength exercise or aerobics training	Run a distance of four miles	Rest day or 30 minutes of Yoga	Run for 20 miles	Rest day
Week Twenty-Two	Cross Training	Run a distance of three miles	Strength exercise or aerobics training	Run a distance of one mile	Rest day	Run for 12 miles	Rest day
Week Twenty-Three	Cross Training	Run a distance of three miles	Strength exercise or aerobics training	4 miles	Rest day	Run for six miles	Rest day

Week Twenty-Four	Cross Training	Run a distance of one mile	Strength exercise or aerobics training	2 miles	Rest day	Race day, run the entire 26.2 miles	Rest day

Marathon!

Chapter 7:

Nutrition and Recovery

Chapter summary

- Healthy nutrition for a marathon

- Macronutrients for training a marathon

- Developing a runner's diet

- Choosing optimum food for race day

- Carbohydrate loading for runners

- Hydration plan

- Rest days

When you run a marathon, you will need to stick to a healthy diet plan in the weeks prior to the run. As you train to run the 26.2 miles, the process leading to race day should include a focus on the best nutrition for race day and for the days when you are training. An important part of this grueling training schedule is planning the nutrition that will fuel the workouts. A suitable diet would essentially provide all the necessary nutrients for your general health, support the taxing physical workouts, and provide energy when you run.

Healthy Nutrition for Marathoners

Marathoners perform the same activity continuously for hours. This puts pressure on the body, particularly on the feet. A lot of runners, however, don't put emphasis on the nutrition side of running. You have the opportunity to optimize your performance in training and on race day if you pay attention to what you eat.

You need to ensure that you eat food that stores enough calories in the body. The primary step is to ensure you are getting sufficient calories that will support your training activities. The risk of muscle loss and stress is high if you fuel the body incorrectly. You could also suffer illness caused by poor sleep.

The International Society of Sports Nutrition (ISSN), a not-for-profit academic society based in the United States of America, recommends the following as you are performing a moderate exercise:

Training period: 5 to 6 weeks

Average weight of the athlete: 110 to 220 pounds

Calorie intake per day: 2000 to 7000

In order to meet this high demand for calories you will need to eat three meals a day and numerous snacks in between those meals. While training, you are advised to select foods that are dense in nutrients and avoid soda and junk food. However, junk food might appear to be the easiest route to acquiring the needed calories. A well-balanced diet is recommended and should include whole-grain starchy foods, lean meats, healthy fats, fruits, and vegetables.

A marathon runner will require a healthy diet that contains carbohydrates, protein, fat, vitamins, minerals, and water. Training to run a marathon will demand high energy expenditure that will require a lot of calories. The calorie quantity required will vary according to your metabolic rate, speed and duration of the run, size of the body, the overall level of activity, and composition of the body.

Relying on Macronutrients For Training to Run In a Marathon

Carbohydrates, proteins, and fats, referred to here as 'macronutrients', are all possible sources of energy; however, the body prefers to lean on fats and carbohydrates. An active athlete is, therefore, advised to take food that is high in carbohydrates and fats.

The marathon diet should be designed focusing on the most important macronutrient, which is carbohydrates. Carbohydrates will provide the body with enough fuel to successfully finish a marathon. A recommendation from ISSN states that for intense training plans, athletes need to eat between five to eight grams per kilogram of bodyweight of carbohydrates per day. Carbohydrates also assist in hydrating the body. The body will store four grams of water for every gram of glycogen stored in the liver and/or muscles.

Protein is an essential nutrient for athletes. A recommendation from ISSN states that, for intense training plans, athletes need to eat between 1.4 and 1.8 grams per kilogram of bodyweight per day.

Recoveries from injury are boosted by protein. Protein also helps build lean muscle mass and aids in the prevention of injury. The intake of protein should be done throughout the day, and it is encouraged to eat a protein-rich meal after the run.

ISSN recommends that an athlete should ensure their diet is composed of about 30% fat, calculated as a percentage of total calories. The amount can vary depending on needs.

Developing a Marathon Training Diet

It is encouraged that while an athlete focuses on the training schedule when preparing to run a marathon, attention must also be put on a solid nutrition plan. Listen to your body, and consume food when you are hungry. Understand why your body is sluggish during the run. It could be caused by not eating enough food, or you may be selecting foods that are not appropriate. Increase the calories you are taking if you are going to be running more than two hours a day. Stick to a plan that calculates calories needed based on the miles that you are running.

Create a balanced meal plan for the training schedule. Ensure the plan slots a proper meal, at latest, three to four hours before you run. One to two hours before the workout, have a snack that is high in either protein or carbohydrates. 45 minutes after the meal, you may have a full meal consisting of protein and carbohydrates to assist the muscles to recover.

Ensure Maximum Nutrition in the Morning, at Midday, and at Dinner Time

Listed below is a plan of the foods necessary for marathon training if you are to achieve your goals:

- Breakfast in the morning: Toasted whole wheat slice, a banana, half an avocado

- Morning snack: Apple

- Lunch: Small bowl of sugar beans, one quarter chicken piece, assorted vegetables, and some lean cheese

- Snack before you run: Low-fat cheese or low-calorie yogurt

- Dinner: Brown rice, lean meat

- Snack at bedtime: Lean milk, whole grain cereals

Choosing the Optimum Food for Race Day

Choosing the proper nutrition for race day is the important final step when you are preparing the training plan. If you choose foods that don't meet the requirements, it can reduce your performance.

Loading Carbohydrates For the Runners

A pre-race joke that goes around is that when you are preparing to participate in a marathon, you will need to eat lots of pasta the night prior to the race. The joke is real because you will need to eat a lot of carbohydrates so that your body can generate maximum energy on race day. Carbo-loading is a process that athletes use in order to perform at their maximum potential. There are, however, a lot of other activities that you will need to perform before carbo-loading. Rather, you will end up upsetting the digestive system or suffer from fatigue when you plan to load food in one meal before the race.

Definition of 'Carbohydrate (Carbo) Loading'

The body prefers to use glycogen in order to fuel its intense activities like running. When you fill up the reserves of glycogen, you are likely to successfully compete at your maximum performance in a marathon race.

Carbo-loading is achieved by eating excess carbohydrates to allow maximum storage of glycogen in the muscles and liver. If the body has, for example, an excess of 2,000 calories stored in the body, it can provide enough fuel to run for approximately two hours before you exhaust the energy. Carbohydrate loading, also referred to as 'carbo-loading', therefore involves the gradual increase of the total starch taken in order to increase glycogen just before you participate in a big race. The glycogen is usually stored in the liver and used by the muscles to give energy to the runner.

One of the major reasons why you should carbo-load is because maintaining higher reserves of carbohydrates will improve your performance during a marathon. When you load carbohydrates, you avoid fainting due to a loss of energy. In racing terms, this is usually termed 'bonking' or 'hitting the wall'. This is when the body runs out of fuel, resulting in cramping of muscles and a reduction in pacing speed.

Athletes who have extra glycogen in their livers will release excess carbs during the race. As explained by nutritionists, when carbohydrates are depleted in the body, the enzymes convert fat into energy. A substance called 'adenosine triphosphate' (ATP) is produced at a slower rate by fat compared to carbohydrates. ATP provides energy for all metabolic processes in the body. The pace will decrease when fat is responsible for the production of energy.

It can be noted that while carbo-loading is certainly necessary for long races that take two or more hours, it will also assist for shorter races.

How to Load Carbohydrates Correctly

In meals that ordinarily have a piece of toast, increase the number of toasts to two. Where you would take half a toast, increase to one whole toast. Replace fat or fiber with carbohydrates in your meals.

Dietary suggestion for correct carbo loading:

Period	Serving portion
Three to four days before the race	Half plate of rice or potatoes A quarter plate of protein A quarter plate of vegetables
Period	Serving Portion
Breakfast on the day of the race	1.5 to 2.5 grams per pound of body weight
Period	Serving Portion
One hour before the race	One carbohydrate rich snack or a banana

Research has shown that an athlete will increase her stored glycogen by 15 percentage points if she eats a meal that is heavy in carbohydrates three hours before the race.

Although carbo-loading can begin at about seven days away from race day, the general practice is to begin three to four days before the race. During this period, you should increase your carb intake while reducing fiber and fats. For half a marathon, the general advice is to start carbo-loading three days before that race.

You need a good, starchy mix that will enhance your meals. The following foods are important when creating a diet for carbo-loading:

- Pasta, vegetables, shrimp

- Rice, chopped apples, goat cheese, chicken piece, salmon,

- Potato, spinach, mushrooms, tomatoes, and mozzarella cheese

You are advised to rely on simple carbohydrates the day before your race.

Eight Big Mistakes People Make When They Carbo-Load

1. Do not consume all the carbs on one occasion. When planning the nutrition for a marathon, avoid slotting a carbo-loading meal for the night before. This will not give the body adequate time to store and digest the carbs. It may also make you a bit sluggish on the morning of the race.

2. You must avoid reducing the reserves of carbs in the body before the main race. Athletes should avoid depleting the carb reserves in their bodies, as it will expose them to the risk of injury.

3. It is not recommended to eat above the normal quantities or above the prescribed carbo-loading levels. High glycogen levels are mostly associated with nervousness before the race and should be avoided.

4. If you gain weight, you do not stress yourself. When you carbo-load, you are likely to gain some weight. It is a result of the extra water absorbed by the excess carbohydrates. Gaining weight during carbo-loading sessions actually serves to show you that you have fueled yourself and you are now ready to run.

5. Avoid taking excessive fiber during the carbo-loading period. Athletes need to stop eating extra fiber, as this can tax the gastrointestinal

system (GI), the system that makes enzymes for digestion. Therefore, instead of eating a white toasted slice, you may replace it with whole wheat toast.

6. You will need to ensure that you plan carbo-loading on your nutrition schedule for the race. You are advised to incorporate carbo-loading in your training plan, especially on days when you perform the long run. This will allow you time to adjust to the carbo-loading plan, and it will not be a new practice when a marathon approaches.

7. Ensure that you consume sufficient carbohydrates to allow the body to reserve. A healthy diet for runners is not necessarily a vegetable regime. You will need carbohydrates to fuel your intensive runs. The formula to use to calculate the required amount of carbs during the carbo-loading period is an intake of eight to 12 grams of carbohydrates for every kilogram of body weight.

8. It is highly recommended that you drink adequate fluids during the carbo-loading period. These four types of starch are used to make glycogen in the body, and they are glucose, fructose, and sucrose. They require different fluids to transport them to the various areas where activities are happening. It is, therefore, important to drink the various liquids that are available, as this will allow the body to utilize the sugars and salts properly.

The Best Hydration Strategy For a Marathon

If you starve for a month, and the climatic conditions are calm to moderate, you will survive. However, if you take away water from a person and place her in a desert, they are likely to die within two days. Oxygen, water, and food are the necessities for living. If you don't drink adequate water, you are likely to suffer a lot of consequences due to dehydration. Because you are dehydrated, your aerobic energy capacity will reduce, which will thereby decrease your training endurance capacity and affect your muscle strength.

How Do You Ensure Adequate Hydration For a Marathon?

The various functions of water can be summarized as:

1. Transporting nutrients to the active tissues.

2. Facilitating waste removal coming from muscle activity.

3. Regulating temperature.

4. Delivering oxygen to tissues.

Performance in a marathon is affected by the body temperature and your hydration patterns during the race. Dehydration poses a lot of dangers during exercise, but overhydration can also be negative. During training and the race, you need to drink a lot of fluids. When you start the race, dehydration begins because close to 75 percent of the energy you expend is transformed to heat which is lost.

The rehydration requirements will vary depending on your sweating rate, the ambient heat, humidity of the environment, and the intensity of the race. You must make drinking water a habit and ensure that you are hydrated at least two days before you run a marathon. Four hours before the race, you should start by drinking approximately 600ml of water. After sipping the water, check the clarity of your urine. Add an extra 400ml if your urine is not transparent. Drinking up to a liter might dilute the sodium balance in the blood, which could increase the need for a bathroom during the race.

Recommended Frequency of Hydration During a Marathon

As alluded to earlier, the amount of recommended water intake varies from one person to another; however, it is ideal to aim to drink between 400ml and 800ml. The amount taken should be adjusted to suit your thirst level, intensity levels, and prevailing ambient conditions.

One of the aspects to be learnt during training is the total amount of fluids that your body requires during intense activities. The formula to calculate the required water is recording your mass before a session, especially on long runs. At the end of the training race, you measure your weight again and calculate the loss in mass during the training session.

The color of your urine is dependent on the amount of water you drink. This is because the yellow pigments in the urine are diluted by fluids. Check the color of your urine against the chart below and use the actual color to determine the amount of water to be taken.

Urine Color Chart

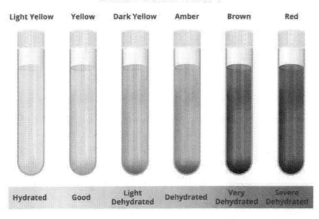

Color of Urine	Verdict	Recommendation
Light Yellow	Hydrated	You are good to run. Enjoy your race
Yellow	Good	You should sip a few milliliters of water, but otherwise, you may run
Dark Yellow	Light Dehydration	Drink a fluid that contains sodium 30 minutes before you run

Amber	Dehydrated	Drink water with sodium salts
Brown	Very Dehydrated	Sip lots of water and sodium
Red	Severe Dehydration	Drink lots of water with sodium

Residual fluid in the stomach is necessary when you run. This will assist with fluid flow in the body throughout the race.

Hyponatremia is a medical condition where the sodium levels in the blood are too low. The body will retain a lot of water due to this condition, and this will dilute the sodium, causing the levels to reduce. Symptoms of hyponatremia include nausea, headaches, confusion, and fatigue.

Plan for Marathon Hydration

Before the marathon, avoid drinking lots of water, as it will elevate the probability of falling into hyponatremia. Take in a drink full of electrolytes the night prior to the marathon so that you may boost the plasma levels in your blood. Two hours before the race, sip two eight ounces of water or a sports drink. This is to allow enough time for the body to absorb the fluids.

During the race, it is advised that you personalize your hydration strategy. This is because our conditions are different, and we lose varying amounts of sodium in our sweat. Just because you see a drink station, does not mean you need to drink. Only stop to drink when it is necessary. The levels of sodium that are recommended in sports juices is 23 milligrams to a maximum of 69 milligrams per deciliter. These levels are sufficient to take care of the intake of electrolytes without having to drink supplements. We usually replace our electrolytes with meals or some salty snacks. If you are on diuretic medication because of hypertension, you might need to increase your intake of electrolytes because you are probably losing more as you run. Some of the symptoms of reduced levels of electrolyte are:

- Feeling confused and being easily irritable.

- Sporadic headaches.

- Resigning to fatigue.

- Diarrhea.

- Feeling constipated.

- Arrhythmia: Irregular or fast heart rate.

- Having muscle cramps, muscle spasms, and body weakness.

- Feeling nauseated and vomiting.

- Numbness or tingling in limbs, fingers, and toes.

Why Are Runners Advised to Program Rest Days in Their Training Plan?

Continuous training assists in improving the performance of an athlete. It might seem a perfect idea not to rest when you are training for a big marathon race. However, if you take some days off, it also helps you to perform well during a race. The following reasons explain why it is necessary to incorporate rest days in your training plan.

Repairing Damage to Muscles

Running will put a lot of pressure on your muscles. The high frequency of long runs while training for a big race, such as a marathon, will further exert more pressure on muscles that will weaken the body fibers. A lot of the repair work to the muscles occurs while you are sleeping and resting. Muscles also strengthen when they are rebuilding themselves. Therefore, you require adequate sleep and enough rest during the day to allow your body to regenerate itself.

Strengthen Your Immune System

Your immune system will be compromised if you exercise frequently and don't give the body adequate rest to repair the muscles. Because inflammation is a response to a failing immune function, the body can no longer fight bacteria, possibly exposing you to ailments such as colds and flu. Falling sick regularly will limit the days that you can train properly without having to retire because the body cannot get over the sickness.

Lessen the Risk of Injury

Excessive running will expose your body to greater chances of injury. It is when you don't allow the body to self-repair that you risk the following injuries that are a result of repeated stress to the body: Ankle sprains, iliotibial band syndrome, and patellofemoral syndrome. One other advantage of rest days, separate from circumventing repeated stress injuries, is that they can assist you to avoid acute injuries. Rest days will also help you reserve energy that will increase your alertness when you train the next day.

Address the Issue of Long-Term Injuries

Rest days allow you to deal with that troublesome, long-standing damage to the body. Giving the injury time to heal is very necessary, as trying to shorten the healing time can be detrimental to your long-term goals of running. You stand a greater chance of running consistently in your life if you allow time to rest. When you take rest, you may utilize mobility aids that are designed to keep you exercising even when you are injured.

Allow the Brain to Take Rest

If you are a recreational runner, you could be part of a group of people who find running relaxing and an avenue to release stress. It will, however, create stress and anxiety if you run continuously without giving your brain rest. The stress hormone, cortisol, can be activated by excessive training in any sport. Cortisol can lead to insomnia, mood swings, and irritability issues. When you allow the body to rest, you will avoid these symptoms and you will feel elation and relaxation.

Experience Greater Benefit: How You Can Make the Most of Rest

Rest Days

To successfully complement your rest days, it is advisable that you integrate the following activities into the days that you take a break:

- Stretch on the floor.

- Use a foam roller to facilitate your stretching.

- Soak yourself in a jacuzzi.

- Immerse yourself in a hot bath.

- Perform light yoga that does not exert stress on the muscles.

- Take in fluids that have adequate salts.

- Relax on a sandy beach.

- Drink plenty of water.

- Get plenty of quality sleep.

If resting is retrogressive and you have to exercise, you are advised to pace slowly without putting a lot of stress on your muscles, and recover your body. Limit yourself to slow-to-moderately-paced walks. It is a form of active recovery from injury.

Chapter 8:

Mind and Body

Chapter overview

- The connection between body and mind

- Hormones responsible for stress reduction

- Effect of running on mood elation

- Improvement of sleep

The Mind and Body Connection

Phrases such as "my blood is boiling", "my gut feel is", or "you are being a pain in my neck", are examples of how the brain can affect the body. The mind is described as an assortment of thoughts, a collection of past experiences, feelings, and beliefs that make up your internal world. There is constant communication between the mind and the body to the extent that it is clear, especially when your physical symptoms are exposed.

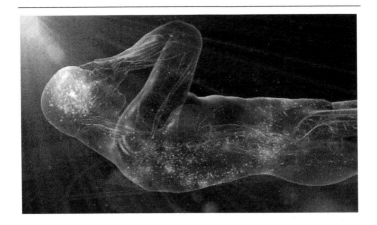

These messages are communicating adjustments that need to be affected to the functioning of the entire body. An example is when you are running and you see a car speeding towards you, the brain will tell the body to move out of the way of a potential accident. The mind is always alert at noticing potential danger and communicates so that your body is safe. When the body is tired, it communicates to the brain the need to sleep. There is, therefore, a close link between the brain and the body. Physical symptoms can affect your feelings, the things you choose to do, and issues that are deliberated in your mind.

Fight-Flight Mechanism

This defense mechanism, also known as the 'acute stress response', is triggered by the release of hormones that include adrenocorticotropic hormone and corticotropin-releasing hormone. The hormones responsible for either fighting a threat or running away from danger are an example of the intimate relationship between the mind and the body. It is an instinctive psychological response to a perceived threat that can be viewed as either frightening or stressful.

Tips for Enhancing the Mind-Body Link for Running

Cultivating a strong link between the mind and the body is important if you want to be a successful runner. It will allow athletes to learn faster and be able to apply lessons learned in training.

yes!

The following methods can be pursued if you want to improve the mind-body connection:

1. Train regularly to gain confidence. Generally, the body will understand its capabilities. Through continuous training, the body will relearn the limits of your physical performance. The body communicates the acquired knowledge as feelings of confidence after you achieve the goal set. The lack of confidence is usually arrived at if you know you have not met your training standards. As an athlete, you will need to train so that you raise your confidence level to the maximum and reduce doubt.

2. Enjoy running. It is when you run happily that your performance soars. The reverse is also true; when training ceases to excite you, it could be a message that you are overtraining. Assess

the level of enjoyment when you train and adjust to suit the mood.

3. Find the formula that works for you. You will not discover a training formula that makes you realize your maximum potential as a runner. When you focus on how your body responds to different training regimes, you will be able to identify the formula that works well for you.

The fundamental factors you will need to watch are:

- Pay attention to the miles that your body can handle in a day and a week.

- Discover the optimal training intensity per session.

- Unearth the weekly routine that works best for your body.

- Allow the experience to teach you. Apply all the lessons you learn along the way for the training to be effective.

The alarm system is a result of stress hormones, such as cortisol and adrenaline, being released. The intensity of running helps in releasing the hormone that assists in the production of endorphins. The delightful, serene, and maybe heavenly, feeling that is felt after running is the primary reason why athletes enroll to participate in intense races. The intensity of marathon running guarantees the production of chemicals known as 'endorphins'.

What Are the Chemicals Called 'Endorphins'?

The pituitary gland releases endorphins when the body is responding to stress and pain. To the layman, they are the body's method of fighting pain. Scientists further narrate that the hormones connect with opiate receptors to minimize pain. Additionally, a lot of other activities have been associated with endorphins release, and these include laughing, childbirth, meditation, and eating spicy food or chocolate. This does not, however, raise the chemicals to the same levels as running.

Intense Running is Necessary to Trigger Endorphins to Release

At low levels of intensity, and usually within the first 30 minutes to 45 minutes of running, your body has not released endorphins. During this low-intensity level, the body releases serotonin and norepinephrine, two other neurotransmitters of the feel-good variety. The early release of these two hormones then triggers the release of endorphins, which occurs after an hour of exercise.

Because endorphins are responses to stress, the body has not been subjected to enough intense pressure to warrant release. The body has to be put under pressure to the point where it anticipates pain for endorphins to be released. However, if you subject your body to excess stress, you may fall into a bad mood.

What Are the Benefits of Raising Endorphins Through Running?

1. The chemicals can assist in reducing the symptoms of anxiety and depression. The increase in endorphins during a marathon can reach such powerful levels that their effect in reducing depression and anxiety can be equated to medication from a physician.

2. It may assist in lowering stress effects. When you run regularly, the high production of endorphins results in the body feeling less pressured by stress levels.

4. You will not risk addiction. Because endorphins production occurs naturally in the body, there is no risk of you being addicted to the chemicals.

Correlation Between Running and Mood Elevation

There is a great deal of evidence that shows that there is a positive relationship between the emotional state of a runner and their level of activity. Many psychologists are resorting to conducting counseling sessions while they walk with the patient. Weir K (2011) encourages strolling with a patient during the therapy session, as it assists the patients to be free and relaxed. Clinical psychologists are now prescribing running as a measure to address mental health.

Enhancing Mood

There are high chances of feeling better after a stressful day when you go run. However, the effects of physical activity are not just short lived; they can go as far as alleviating long lasting depression. There is clinical data that confirms that when a person is active, he is less depressed than when he lives a sedentary life. When you commit yourself to training, endorphins and serotonin are released into the body. The two hormones enhance mood, memory, and the ability to learn. Maintaining an active lifestyle is encouraged, since depression is also prevalent in people who start an exercise program and then stop.

Because there is a positive relationship between diabetes and obesity, it seems logical that an exercise prescription could be used to treat mood swings in such patients. The mood boost from exercising gives a diabetic patient some near and instant gratification.

Preventing Anxiety Disorders

Clinical psychologists have toyed around with the idea of using exercise as a remedy for treating, and maybe preventing, anxiety disorder. Anxiety usually triggers a flight or fight response. The nervous system quickly rushes into action, triggering a barrage of reactions such as the pumping of the heart, sweat dripping, feeling dizzy, and panic disorder. Exposing patients to running can complement other medicines in treating these symptoms.

Reduction of Stress Level

When you finish running, a biochemical called 'endocannabinoids' is released in your body. The chemical is transported to the brain through the movement of blood. The chemical is likened to cannabis and has got the similar effect of inducing calmness and a feeling of lessened stress.

Assists You to Recover From Mental Health Challenges

Scientific studies have proved that if you run regularly, you might feel relief from depression and anxiety. Running is, therefore, being used by physicians as therapy and recovery to lessen some of the symptoms of mental illness.

Improves Sleep

When you run, the body produces chemicals that relax the body and help to improve your sleeping schedule by encouraging deep sleep. Sleeping regularly and deeply is important for the brain and a healthy mindset. Running ensures you get a good sleep by increasing your body temperature by a few degrees. A reduction in temperature later on during the day will trigger drowsiness that will assist you in sleeping better.

Negative Effects of Running

Excessive running can result in many ill-effects on your mental health. Running may result in the following:

- Risk of injury to the body.

- In extreme cases, running can be detrimental to the heart, especially if you have a condition.

- Some rare cases of cardiac arrest as a result of running have been reported.

- Addiction to running can interfere with your life by leading to excessive weight loss through over-exercising.

Chapter 9:

Use Visualization in Order

to Run Successfully

Chapter outline

- Engaging all five senses when you visualize

- Creating images of the running processes

- Importance of music to the runner

- Ways to visualize marathon success

The physical body preparation for races is the usual focus of marathoners. That is to be understood because the races exert a lot of physical pressure on the body. Nevertheless, mental preparation will assist you in meeting the goals that you have set to achieve. Visualization in running a marathon is a process where the runner imagines the processes from training to race day.

All your senses of sight, touch, smell, hearing, and taste are involved in this process. Engage all five senses and make a draft of everything that you want from running. Keep updating the draft by including more sensory images as they come to your mind. As the details expand, you will feel like the experience is real.

Creating images of the training periods and the race days is a technique that is used by many successful athletes. According to Strycharczyk & Clough (2015), some of the benefits of visualization are positive thinking methods and instinctive behavior. Many successful athletes have turned to the technique of visualization in order to renew their mental awareness and increase their confidence levels.

The challenge with most people is that they visualize the negative outcomes of a race. Negative thoughts might demotivate you. The mind is the safest place that you may play through potentially challenging situations. A set of difficult actions that improve skills and that can assist in handling highly demanding circumstances can be rehearsed in the brain before the event.

- Elements that you will need to picture in the environment include the race course, the sound of the start gun, and race contestants.

- Create images of a calm environment; a committed picture of yourself relative to competitors.

- Picture yourself together with friends on race day, in a relaxed mood, and in advanced race preparations.

- See yourself in control of the race and being confident that you will run successfully.

- Imagine yourself in a relaxed mood and ready to run.

- Picture successful milestones along the racecourse.

Listening to Music While Running

You will derive some benefits to your performance if you listen to music during physical activity. Music can help to motivate runners to push an extra mile or increase their speed by a few miles per hour. It can also assist the athlete to remain focused by limiting distractions on the track.

Apart from enjoying tunes, music can provide positive benefits on the running course when you are training and during the event. The positive outcomes include:

- An improvement in the mood of the athlete.

- A reduction in distractions from external situations.

- An increase in the performance measurement statistics.

Your mood during the run might positively improve when you listen to a new music genre, a new track, or that favorite track from years gone by. Serotonin is a chemical that is responsible for taking messages from the nerves of our bodies to the brain. The chemical controls a lot of human functions such as our emotions, sleeping, wound healing, and bone health. Listening to music can increase the levels of serotonin in the brain, thereby helping your mood during training and the race.

Throughout the intense routine of exercise, mental fatigue and physical exhaustion are likely to set in. The lungs will start to fight for air, muscle fatigue will set in, and the brain will be contemplating, "I need to stop running, this is enough." Music can assist you to prevent your mind from paying attention to these interruptions caused by exhaustion.

According to a study conducted by Bonnette et al. in 2012, listening to music while you are running improves physical exertion and performance. Runners who listen to music while running tend to run at a higher rate than those who do not. This could be a result of effectively deceiving the brain to turn attention away from fatigue and focus on the lyrics of the music.

Compile a Playlist for Your Running

You will need to determine your running rate, measured in beats per minute, or 'bpm'. This will allow you to align the tempo of your music to your natural running rate.

The following methods can be used in determining the running rate in bpm:

- Practice at your natural pace while on a treadmill. Running at an easy pace on the machine will limit disruptions because you can control the environment.

- Working with a fellow runner, allow your partner to record the time, on a stopwatch, it takes you to complete a single run of 60-80% of maximum heart range.

- Calculate the average time it takes for you to run, and record the time as your standard time in running at a natural pace.

Selecting the Correct Headphones

Because of the high intensity of a marathon, you will be advised to select wireless headphones. This will reduce the risk that when you accidentally drop the earphone, the cables can split from the ear plug due to the intensity of the run. Identifying equipment that will fit comfortably can be just as vital as selecting suitable shoes for the race course.

You are advised to consider the following factors when choosing the best headphones for the marathon:

- The physical structure of the headphones should allow you to wear them in the ear, also known as 'in-ear' models. This earbud or ear hook model is ideal for rough exercise since they fit comfortably and they are firm.

- The quality of sound should enhance your performance. Your mood and emotional connection to the race may be affected negatively by the poor sound quality.

- Choosing headphones with short battery life can affect the maintenance of sound quality.

- The in-ear models, like the ear hook or the earbuds, can be heavy for the ears or the neck. Assess whether the chosen equipment does not put stress on the head before selecting.

Stay Safe by Blocking Out Any Disruptions When Running

Some of the helpful tips to follow when you run while listening to music are listed below:

- Ensure safety by wearing the headphones properly.

- Avoid headphones that cancel noise, and ensure you are alert to any heavy traffic and crowds.

- Use headphones that have a reflection, especially early in the morning or at dawn when the sun is setting.

- Locate a running group. This can help in releasing stress, alleviating any anxiety you feel, and giving you a sense of protection.

- Maintain a safe volume throughout the running, as high volumes may damage your hearing.

- It is important to be aware of what is happening in the surrounding areas you will be running. It is important that you manage the sound volume.

Four Ways That You Can Visualize Success in a Marathon

- Create a collage of images in your mind. One of the tools useful in visualization is a collage that portrays your training and previous successful performance. A collage is defined as a collection of art showing the athlete's movement throughout the training and marathon. The collage can be created on paper or as an application on the computer. The collection will be images of your planned training, pictures of your expected feelings, and your projected success.

- Talk to people in order to connect with the experience. If you're a beginner in running marathons, visualizing the race could be a challenge. In this situation, you are encouraged to network with people that have participated successfully in marathons. If you talk to experienced runners, they will help you create images of the event. In addition to that, you can watch past race videos and listen to podcasts on long-distance running.

- Record goals on index cards. Record your marathon ambitions on index cards. Create an index card for every goal. Recite the goals to yourself every day and with your eyes closed, picture what attaining your targets appears like.

- Make use of a fitness coach. You can conduct guided visualizations under the supervision of a fitness coach. Tools that you are able to access can be online platforms, meditation applications, and others.

- Record questions in a weekly journal. Keep a journal of questions with you and visualize the answers in real life. Examples of questions can be:

  o How will your ideal race day look like, from start to finish?

  o Which songs will be on my playlist?

  o At what times will I play the music?

  o How do I visualize my energy level in the morning?

  o What will I be wearing on race day?

  o Who will run next to me?

- What is my average time in a marathon, and do I want to improve it?

- What will I be drinking and at what points during the race?

- What will I be eating on marathon day, including snacks during the race?

- What deodorant will I be smelling?

- What will I be feeling on the day of the race?

- What will the race environment look like?

- How will I develop my race, from start to finish?

- What will my energy levels be at the start of the race?

- How will I pose at the end of the race?

The vital point to conceptualize would be that the brain needs a proper training strategy. You will require patience to meditate and picture the perceived events. Allow yourself to visualize a positive outcome of the race. Focus all your senses on the visualization processes.

Chapter 10:

Ways to Prevent Burnout

Chapter overview

- Fueling your enthusiasm

- Breaking the marathon into manageable distances

- Definition of 'clutter'

- Decluttering the mind

'Longevity' is the perfect word to describe the relationship that must exist between a runner and their performance in races. Physical injury, stress, and burnout, however, will always threaten the extent to which a runner can sustain a lengthy season. You may reduce stress by striking a workable balance between training, work, and family. A training program that is balanced can help to minimize the risk of physical injury.

Strategies that help in finding joy in training and the excitement to participate in a grueling marathon are necessary approaches to sustaining you in a long season. If you learn to recover from difficult times, it will fuel your enthusiasm and help you avoid burnout in running.

The yearly marathon calendar is usually set out just before the beginning of the year by many running clubs. Once you have a look at the calendar, you are advised to select a blend of smaller races and around three major races in a year.

Setting Goals that are Achievable

If you are a runner of credibility, you will be setting out to enjoy the process of running and the training methods that lead up to race day. Setting sound goals that are within your range should be the first step to a long season of running. If you pick too many races you might be demotivated as your body suffers from fatigue and race monotony. You are advised to set training goals, as they will make you focus on the short-term goals before you set yourself to achieving bigger goals.

1. Break the Total Distance into Time Chunks

Rather than targeting to run miles, breaking the distance into manageable chunks of minutes will make the total mileage doable. The choice of the specific time chunks will depend on your preferences and the pace breakdown.

An examples of time chucks that you may use is outlined below:

Race Miles	Equivalent time chunks
5 miles	30 minutes
6 miles	25 minutes
7 miles	26 minutes
8 miles	27 minutes
6.2 miles	Around 20 minutes

During your exercise drills, you may use the time interval in order to check yourself. You punctuate the run with small walking periods or switch to the playlist and allow time to regroup.

2. Allow Breaks to Coincide with the Times You Refuel

Fuel breaks are necessary because they give you time to boost your energy, time to talk to friends, and time to have that one snack you love. The breaks assist you to interrupt the monotony of pacing. Strategies to refuel will vary, but usually in a marathon, you will need to eat something every 30 to 45 minutes

Impt

3. Make the Water Stations Miniature Finishing Lines.

When you target to reach the next water station, the running will seem easily achievable as opposed to aiming to get to the finish line, which is further up the race course. You can feel motivated by targeting to hydrate your body at the next water point.

4. Divide the Marathon into Segments that are Pace-Based

This works for me! Have done it with 10k race!

The recommended strategy is to gradually pick up the pace, starting with a slow pace and building up to a higher speed. This will prevent the body from burning out at the start of the race and allows you to finish stronger. Run the first five miles at a slower pace, gradually pick the speed at the next 10 miles, and then reach peak speed on the home stretch.

Ways to Declutter your Life

While clutter is usually associated with mercilessly putting items in the environment, untidiness may also happen in the mind. Your mind is regarded as a cluttered mind when it does any of the following:

- does not stop pondering on challenges.

- focuses on negative issues.

- does not stop to worry about negative issues that are outside of its control.

- embraces negative thoughts.

- does not leave experiences.

- holds on to past hurts, including resentments.

- embraces anger for long periods.

- keeps a list of things to be addressed.

- keeps wondering about incomplete goals or dreams.

- allows external distractions.

- permits persistent sensory input into the brain.

If your mind gets muddled up with any of the above, it will waste energy and time on unproductive issues. This will, unfortunately, generate mental distraction, disorganization, confusion, and disorder that will prevent you from focusing on important issues in your life. If your brain is confused, you will be absent from your location, which will prevent you from properly connecting to the moment. Additionally, you will be divorced from the environment you are presently in, and this might negatively affect your relationships.

Once your mind is in this mode, you will need to let the mental habits that are preventing you from reaching your full potential leave your mind. In order to declutter the mind, you will need to pursue intentional behavior that is focused on strengthening the mind's muscles and clearing the confusion. Correct behavior is necessary if you want to clear complex thinking patterns which will not help you solve the challenges and will not assist in clearing your cluttered mind. Focusing on the time you spend on the issues and channeling energy correctly will assist you in overcoming the challenges.

Listed below are fifteen guidelines to support you in clearing your brain and decluttering your mind.

1. Learn to retire to bed and obtain a good sleep. Sleeping has got several advantages that include the benefit of assisting you with a healthy mental state. When you don't get sleep, it is usually a result of somnolence, but it can also be the result of failing to think straight or lack of the ability to recall anything. Research has shown that if you are deprived of sleep, your cells are deprived of the ability to talk to each

other, causing memory lapses. The first step to decluttering your mind is to ensure you get restful sleeping time. Sleeping needs to be a habit; something you do every day.

2. You need to create time to meditate. Meditating is creating time during which you can think over the issues that are occupying your mind and allow time for your mind to clear. You will not be able to declutter your mind from those challenges if you get stuck in your mind. When you focus on practicing meditation, clarity of the mind becomes natural and effortless. Once you contemplate, you will assist in lessening the misunderstanding by adopting your priorities and paying attention to issues while reducing distraction. You will need to practice meditation and create an everyday routine so that you assist your brain to clear the confusion.

3. Learn to transfer your feelings to paper. The other best method to declutter the mind is to record your thoughts in a diary or notebook. All those ideas that are lingering in your brain must be taken away from the mind by jotting them down. Writing your opinions on paper assists in getting them out of your brain because it permits you to get rid of the responsibility to remember them because you have decluttered your mind in the process of recording them. When your brain constantly brainstorms ideas, it might be necessary to quickly jot them so that you may avoid forgetting them. It is also an easy method of storing and managing your ideas. In

order to set aside a place to store ideas quickly, you may develop an application on your phone or carry a notebook with you wherever you go. This will assist you to create some extra headspace that moves around with you. The primary aim is getting space to immediately record an idea as it comes.

4. Keep a journal of your thoughts. Pondering your thoughts can be avoided if you list your feelings and thoughts on paper. You, however, have some options for alleviating the meditative mind. For example, if you are brainstorming on solutions to an issue that is worrying your mind, you might have not managed to pin down a solution, the easiest step is to record everything in a journal. This helps in clearing the mental space and assists in recording personal beliefs to a solution. Journaling can be explained as a way to explore possible solutions in writing and can be a great way for you to ponder on ways to solve the challenges. According to researchers, journaling can assist in treating the mental health of runners. It can assist you in arranging your thoughts and your understanding of the emotions that are affecting you. This is a healthy practice that helps your general wellbeing.

5. Arrange all your priorities. The list of your priorities could be long to the extent that you might struggle to find a correct starting point to solving them. As soon as you dump by jotting down the key deliverables on paper, you may

begin to classify them in order of importance. When you tackle the challenges according to urgency, you may further need to address issues that will create serious negative reparations, like paying an important bill, taking medication, and meeting rigid deadlines of a project. Keeping an eye on the value of your priorities as you deal with them and adjusting the rankings as there are changes is important. The ultimate relief comes when you overcome and cross them off of the list.

6. Reduce multitasking. By nature, humans love performing many tasks at one time. While on the surface, multitasking may seem efficient, it, however, can reduce the efficiency of your ability to complete tasks, thereby burdening the mind with unresolved issues. In order to avoid mental overload, focus must be placed on completing one task at a time. You may measure the time you want to take to complete a certain task, and thus manage your tasks efficiently, as you go about eradicating them from your mind.

7. Train your mind to operate decisively. Mental clutter can be viewed as decisions that have been delayed by you. Life, by definition, may be regarded as being a sequence of choices. Some of the decisions you make might be simple, while others could be complicated to the extent of stirring up emotions, resulting in you putting the decisions to a later date. Rather, procrastination is considered as being one the

biggest causes of confusion of the mind because the brain gets overwhelmed by the numerous decisions that you are putting off to a later date. Paralysis of the process of making decisions may be caused to a greater extent by your over-analysis of the solutions to the challenges. A lot of "what ifs" may constantly bombard your mind, resulting in further clutter.

8. Contest your negative emotions. Negative thinking can incapacitate you by taking up space in your brain. Carrying a sad and disappointed attitude can magnify your misfortunes by twisting real situations. The primary thing to follow is the knowledge that you may talk to yourself to resolve issues that occupy your mind. You need to stop victimizing yourself and redirect those thoughts in a positive way towards talk that is not toxic. Red flags can include thoughts such as, "Poor me," "I cannot complete this marathon," and "I will embarrass my wife." In order to counter that thinking, internalize the idea of challenging yourself. Counter the thoughts by creating arguments like, "Is this thinking correct?" or "I am not distorting my thoughts." It is usually when you convince yourself that the adverse self-talk is wrong that you will begin to think positively about solutions to the challenges. That shift in your mind clears the heavy feeling, the clutter, and confusion, giving you a more positive mindset and a brain free of burden. If you start by acquiring positive experiences you will begin to overcome the challenges of thinking

negatively. As a runner, incorporate a training program that includes practicing gratitude and companionship by making the life of someone in your community better. When you feel you are catching a negative feeling, just identify a need that is close to you; that way, your brain can convert negative thoughts to positive ones.

9. Plan time to worry. It is quite normal to worry about the fears that visit our minds from time to time. The problem is letting the worries consume our mind to a point where it affects our life. If you start to second guess solutions and start rehearsing the same issues in your mind, it will not assist you in any way because you might begin crowding your mind with hypothetical solutions. A runner should plan time to reflect, say, 10 minutes a day, when letting everything out and avoid holding on to the issues. Respect your training program if you have included the worrying minutes in the plan. Do not try to meditate outside the time set aside for pondering. This will assist in decongesting the mind.

10. Allow loved ones to know. Sharing the burden with your partner and/or friends will help lighten it. If you are a novice to running, you might find it necessary to confide in a therapist, an athletics coach, or a more experienced runner so that you may receive professional advice. Off-loading your feelings and mood can assist you in acquiring a clearer viewpoint and breaking the sequence of meditating. This can

help you to ease the burden of carrying the challenges in your mind.

11. Rearrange your surroundings. The chaos that comes with an environment that is cluttered, be it your home or workspace, will make you lose focus. This disorder will constantly draw your attention to useless things and confine your capability to process information correctly and pay attention to issues at hand. A cluttered environment will unnecessarily occupy your mind. It will create a cloudy mind by blocking the ability to think clearly and act properly in situations. It is only when you declutter that you can improve the physical state of your mind.

12. Take time to enjoy nature. When you feel heavy, take time to wander outside, seeing birds, animals, and if you can, the general green sight of the environment. It will help you to fight mental health issues by decreasing the level of depression. Nature restores the mind, refreshes the body, gives you a boost of energy, and reinvigorates your mind.

13. Social media can be depressing. Limit your access to it. Social media will add to the brain clutter in you. This can have a negative effect on mental health because it can increase the feeling of loneliness and depression. Limit the amount of time you spend on social media; your mind might acquire feelings triggered by sensitive information coming from the social platforms. If your mind starts getting cluttered

by social media issues, it could be time to break from it.

14. Take time to exercise. As discussed elsewhere in this manuscript, running improves your physical being and mind. Training for a marathon decreases anxiety, helps with depression, allows the mind to concentrate when solving issues, and generally relaxes the muscles. We all know exercise is good for your overall wellbeing, including both your body and your mind. In addition to decreasing anxiety and depression, regular exercise can help you concentrate and feel mentally sharp for the tasks at hand.

15. Unwind by taking a break. At the end of it all, each person requires time and space to wind down. It can be a week-long vacation or even 10 minutes spent relaxing and not doing anything. The goal is, however, not to empty your mind, but to limit your thinking to manageable issues. Decluttering helps you in making life simple, allows you the opportunity to build new mental habits, provides clarity of thought, and makes you an organized person.

Conclusion

In conclusion, the book demonstrates that your body is a machine that can be adapted to running a marathon. As a machine, the body requires maintenance. It needs food to fuel all the functions necessary for living. If you embrace the correct mindset, your body can adjust from holding the television remote while sitting on the couch to training to run a grueling 26.2-mile race. You may begin to train at any stage of your life. What is critical is to maintain consistency in training while paying attention to the goals that took you to participate in a marathon.

Every individual is built to run. The design of our bodies was perfectly created to transform us into active and enduring runners. Our hips and feet are shaped correctly to run, and the long legs and the shock-absorbing spinal discs make it possible for us to move forward with intensity. The ability of our bodies to regulate heat by sweating allows our bodies to accommodate rigorous activities such as running. It is, therefore, not surprising that running in a marathon can be strongly linked with numerous advantages to the body and the mind.

It can be difficult to adjust to running if you are a beginner or you are coming from a long layoff. In these instances, running can be extremely brutal to the body. However, once you get into the groove of it, you will enjoy the blissful life, the opportunity to meditate, and the sense of freedom that comes with running.

Training to run in a marathon and participating in a marathon will significantly improve your physique and brain. Being a form of aerobic exercise, marathon running is able to lessen the effects of stress, allow recovery of the heart, and assist in alleviating the warning signs of depression.

Why Running Will Benefit You

Some researchers have proved that people benefit from running because we integrate running into our lives. Exercise alone has been considered as a miracle drug by many physicians. Being the most accessible form of aerobic exercise, running is the simplest form of training. What's more, it is not expensive.

Running is an aerobic fitness exercise that complements the health of the heart in many ways. In addition, marathon races assist in burning calories, strengthening the heart muscle, and firming up the other muscles of the body. The list of psychological benefits gained by runners from the sport is long.

It is always important to remember you are running for the fun of it. People who have successfully completed marathons will tell you that it is when you run for fun that the race gets exciting.

A training program of just 30-minute runs can assist in lessening the symptoms of depression and mood recovery. If you spend 30 minutes on a treadmill, it is enough to lift your mood if you are suffering from a major disorder of depression. Studies have shown that even a walk of 30 minutes can yield the same benefits.

Running can significantly improve cardiovascular health. If you just run five minutes a day, you are likely to add more years to your life. Research has shown that aerobic activity is generally good for the health of the heart. Cardiovascular fitness can, therefore, be improved by running in a marathon.

Contrary to popular belief, running in a marathon appears to improve knee health. If you have knee pain, it could be an indication that you are overtraining or a sign that you need to improve your flexibility, and the injury might cause you to rest. However, running might not be the cause of the knee injury. Running will also control the body-to-mass index (BMI) by strengthening the body and the bones. The BMI is basically a ratio of the weight of your body compared to your height. The ratio is used to screen the categories of masses that may lead to health challenges such as diabetes and heart problems. The disadvantage with using the index is that the weight factor might be misleading as it does not separate fat from muscle.

In young people, running assists with mood improvement, including boosting the ability to focus on life challenges. In children and young adults, running improved their focus, helped their working memory, and improved the ability to switch tasks.

Research has indicated that running can assist in keeping the mind healthy as you grow old (Lin T and Kuo Y 2013). For aging adults, there is a long list of cognitive benefits, including memory improvement, focus, and enhanced ability to switch tasks.

Resistance to stress can be improved by running. It has been shown by research that any aerobic exercise improves the ability of an individual to cope with stress. Training triggers some resistance to stress. This could be due to the fact that aerobic exercise surges the levels of neurotransmitters, such as serotonin, that may cause the brain to produce new neurons.

A marathon could be the best way to burn calories.

Weight of individual in pounds	Calories burned
130	608
150	701
170	794
190	888
210	981

230	1075

An average individual will burn, on average, between 80 and 140 calories for every mile run. However, the total calories that are burned is highly dependent on the weight of the person, the intensity of the exercise, and time spent running.

Running will significantly decrease your probability of illness. Individuals who run are significantly less likely to develop a number of forms of cancer.

Holistic Approach to Running

If you are a novice, this manuscript has demonstrated to you that running is a progressive sport that can suit even the beginner. One exciting aspect you will enjoy is seeing how you progress from struggling to complete one mile to effortlessly running through the finish line of 26 miles. Marathon beginners usually start by making a lot of mistakes, such as adding too many miles to the training plan, creating an unstructured exercise plan, skipping the cross training, and not fueling properly.

When you adopt a holistic approach, you examine all aspects of running life and ensure that there is nothing that can distract you from the schedule. Strategically ignoring the statistics, such as the miles you run and the speed, might make you a sustainable and enduring runner. You will need to focus beyond the numbers and pay attention to a whole range of targets that come with a successful training program.

The following areas should occupy your mind on this exciting journey to competing in a marathon:

- Do you want to lose weight?

- Could this be a plan to meditate?

- Do you want to tone your body?

- Is your body out of shape?

- Do you want to strengthen your muscles?

- Do you have an uncontrollable hunger to complete a marathon?

- Do you crave the health benefits that come with training to run a marathon?

It is essential to understand the reasons you are competing in a race of 26 miles. Whatever the reasons, you will need to define your goals for running in a marathon quite clearly. You may stick to the goals in important areas like the bathroom, the kitchen, and the bedroom. It will motivate you to keep running when the wet winter arrives or when your muscles start to give in to stress and pain. If your reasons change, update them, but ensure that they align to your running purpose. Remember that running is a competing priority; it might be overtaken by others.

References

Akyurt E (2016) https://pixabay.com/photos/food-break-noon-evening-noodle-4220382/

Anccapictures   (2015)
    https://pixabay.com/users/anncapictures-
    1564471

Carvalho   De   L   (2016)
    https://pixabay.com/illustrations/girl-universe-
    fantasy-galaxy-space-5801511/

Delineates J (2020) https://pixabay.com/photos/man-
    headphones-smile-happy-music-6159967/

file:///C:/Users/DELL/Desktop/TUW_Marathon/M
    ental%20Toughness%20in%20Marathon.pdf

ISSN exercise & sport nutrition review: research &
    recommendations
    https://jissn.biomedcentral.com/articles/10.11
    86/1550-2783-7-7

Kapa65   (2013)   https://pixabay.com/photos/lion-
    proudly-beautiful-maul-teeth-685134/

(Lin T and Kuo Y 2013), Exercise Benefits Brain
    Function: The Monoamine Connection Brain
    Sci.   2013,   3,   39-53.
    https://doi.org/10.3390/brainsci3010039

Lortie   C   (2019)
file:///C:/Users/DELL/Desktop/TUW_Mara
thon/Ten_simple_rules_for_better_runni

nhttps://www.frontiersin.org/article/10.3389/fspor.20
21.735220/full.pdf

Ohlaman P (2015)

Scapin   https://pixabay.com/photos/marathon-
running-sport-jogging-1529149/

Sember V & Morrison S (2018), Differences in Physical
Activity and Academic Performance between
Urban and Rural Schoolchildren in Slovenia
Medical Journal of Sports Science and Medicine

Strycharczy D & Clough P (2017) *Developing Mental
Toughness: Coaching strategies to improve performance,
resilience and wellbeing* University of Huddersfield
https://pure.hud.ac.uk/en/publications/develo
ping-mental-toughness-coaching-strategies-to-
improve-perfor

Wal_172619   (2019)
https://pixabay.com/photos/marathon-
enthusiasm-running-clap-4631297/

Stewardesign   (2016)
https://pixabay.com/users/stewardesign-
7115679/

Uveese (2016) https://pixabay.com/photos/barefoot-
barefoot-running-feet-2521931/

Rembowski A https://pixabay.com/photos/zumba-marathon-sport-exercise-4333580/

https://www.istockphoto.com/en/photo/senior-adult-african-american-man-crossing-finish-line-during-marathon-gm1053565558-281490468?phrase=marathon%2Bgoals

https://www.istockphoto.com/photo/young-beautiful-woman-drinking-water-during-morning-jogging-in-the-park-gm1433210823-475210297?utm_source=pixabay&utm_medium=affiliate&utm_campaign=SRP_image_spons ored&utm_content=https%3A%2F%2Fpixaba y.com%2Fimages%2Fsearch%2Fmarathon%25 20food%2F%3Fmanual_search%3D1&utm_ter m=marathon+food

Placidplace   (2022)
         https://pixabay.com/illustrations/humanoid-human-brain-technology-7230898/

Made in the USA
Las Vegas, NV
11 July 2023

74475037R00109